TASTEMAKER

TASTEMAKER

Cooking with Spice, Style & Soul

SCOT LOUIE

weldon**owen**

FOR ZELDA

CONTENTS

INTRODUCTION 8

STAY READY 11

OH, WOW SPICE
SUBSTITUTIONS 13

COCKTAILS 15

Brunch Punch 17

Smoke & Berry 18

Sorrel Margarita 21

Paloma-Ann 22

Basil Spritz 23

Jamaican Rum Punch 25

Tamarind Margarita 26

Island Ting 28

Yard Toddy 29

Tea-Tini 30

BREAKFAST & BRUNCH 33

Toasted Brioche with Cream
Cheese & Strawberry Compote 35

Baked Egg Bread Bowl 36

Chickpea Cook-up 38

Breakfast Pockets 39

Honey Butter Cornbread Waffle 41

Callaloo & Saltfish Fritters 42

Breakfast Casserole 44

Jammy Eggs & Honey Butter Toast 45

APPETIZERS & ALL-DAY MEALS 47

Chorizo Taco Cups 49

Garlic Lemon Pepper Wings 50

Jerk Chicken Burrito 52

Mason Jar Noodle Soup 53

Bougie Chopped Cheese Sliders 55

Sticky Fried Short Ribs 56

Caesar Toast 57

Caramelized Shallot & Roasted
Garlic Lobster Bisque 59

Hot Honey Crispy Shrimp 60

Elevated Snack Wraps 62

Mustard Chicken Bites 63

Crab Rangoon Dip 65

DINNERPLUS 67

Oven Jerk Chicken 68

Sausage & Sun-Dried Tomato
Stuffed Shells 71

Creamy Scallop Pappardelle 73

Jerk Mac & Cheese with
Creamy Jerk Sauce 75

Jamaican Rice & "Peas" 77

Sweet Sausage Smash Burger 78

Jamaican Oxtail 81

Brown Stew Chicken 83

Chicken Meatballs with Garlic
Butter Sauce & Orzo Salad 84

One-Pan Maple Chicken & Rice 85

Jump-Start Chicken 87

Rasta Risotto 88

Brown Butter Tortellini	89	SOMETHING SWEET	129
Gochujang Crab Noodles	90	Strawberry Cheesecake Cookies	131
BBL Fried Cabbage	93	S'mores Dip	132
Three Sauce Naan Pizza with Crispy Prosciutto	95	Pear Spice Cake with Bourbon Glaze	134
Turmeric-Ginger Branzino	96	Creamy No-Bake Cheesecake Bites	135
Garlicky Lemon Pepper Lamb Chops with Honey Glaze	99	Salted Caramel Pretzel Blondies	136
Soul Bowl Series	100	Blueberry-Compote Butter-Crunch Cake	139
Collard Kale with Smoked Turkey-Neck Broth	102	Crispy Cornflake Squares	140
Holy Trinity Rice	103	Biscuit Doughnuts with Lemon Glaze	141
Roasted Sweet Potatoes	104		
Black-Eyed Peas	105	SAUCES, DRESSINGS & GARNISHES	142
Creamy Cajun Chicken	106	Ginger Simple Syrup	143
		Creamy Jerk Sauce	145
GOOD & GUILT FREE	109	Garlic Butter Sauce	146
Boosted Breakfast Bowl	111	Roasted Garlic Cesar Dressing	147
Cauliflower Southwest Skillet with Chipotle Sauce	112	Sun-Dried Tomato Aioli	149
Callaloo Stew	115	Perfect Roasted Garlic	150
Orzo Salad	116	Scotch Bonnet Aioli	151
Lemongrass Ground Turkey	117	Strawberry Compote	152
Spinach & Artichoke Zucchini Boats	118	Chipotle Sauce	155
Steak-Wrapped Asparagus	121	Jamaican Green Seasoning	156
Cucumber Crab Rounds	122	Seafood Stock	158
Grilled Halloumi Salad with Tahini Dressing	123	Chicken Stock	159
Zucchini & Green Onion Fritters	125	INDEX	160
Jamaican Steamed Cabbage	126	ACKNOWLEDGMENTS	167
Garlic-Ginger Bok Choy	127		

INTRODUCTION

Oh, wow!—I'm writing these first few words on the heels of turning thirty, and I can't believe this is my reality. My love for food and eating is finally paying off—insert audience cheering—and I'm happy to welcome you into my kitchen through the pages of this book.

Tastemaker is a love letter to my blended Jamaican–New York roots. This cook-at-home handbook is a beautiful blend of Jamaican and Soul Food cuisine. It is a thank you to my supporters, and a welcome to my new readers. Consider *Tastemaker* the reason you'll want to cook at home more often. Trying these recipes will expose you to a whole new world of tasty, mouthwatering, and aesthetically pleasing meals. You'll find recipes that are familiar, yet fabulous—whether it's classic Southern mac and cheese with a Jamaican twist or a New York deli staple that's elevated enough for your next dinner party.

Throughout my life, the kitchen has been my safe space, my go-to, where some of my most fond memories were made—because food has always been the center of my world, even before fashion was. Growing up watching my mom, grandmother, and my seven aunts and uncles cook was one of my favorite things to do, aside from eating. My late grandmother Zelda taught me the importance of sifting flour and burning curry, which shaped the cook I am today.

I remember that during my junior year of high school, when I was trying to figure it all out—SATs, getting a car, college plans, sexuality, Lady Gaga's meat dress, the Kardashians—the most important question was "What is next for me?" I had already been climbing the styling career ladder (less than a year later I would graduate high school and land Lil' Kim as a client). While styling and fashion were exciting to me, I had no interest in going to college to study fashion. I presented the idea of going to culinary school to my Jamaican mother, Patricia (whom I love dearly)—she wasn't going for it. So, off to California I went to chase a future in celebrity fashion.

Weight has never been an issue for me, but my weight has always been an issue for others. My mother's response to culinary school was "No, you'll eat too much and get fatter." Over the years, I've worked hard both personally and professionally to remove the stigma associated with enjoying eating. The exploration of food and cooking is exciting and expands knowledge. Food is how we nourish, how we gather, and how we reminisce. While I absolutely encourage choosing healthy options, there shouldn't be any negative association with tasteful indulgences or the exploration of cuisines.

Living in California was the first time I had ever had guacamole, and I know what you're thinking, but Chipotle wasn't a big thing for me growing up in Brooklyn with a Jamaican family—after all, we call avocados "pears" and eat them with bulla cake. As the years have progressed, my palate has expanded well beyond California guacamole. My styling business, wonderful clients, and personal travels have afforded me the opportunity to dine in cities like Paris, Tulum, Miami, San Francisco, Puerto Morelos, Punta Cana, and Auckland.

Scot Louie from Brooklyn, New York, whose favorite meal was (and still might be) four chicken wings fried hard and chopped up with pork fried rice, now also loves pan-seared scallops in brown butter and a wood-oven pizza with arugula and prosciutto. My love for food inspired me to start an Instagram account that many now know as DinnerPlus, a self-proclaimed food board across all social platforms. I decided to create DinnerPlus Spices by Scot Louie and have launched five unique blends: DinnerPlus Whitespice, Yardspice, Cajunspice, Zestyspice, and Brining Blend. These spice blends are essentials in my kitchen and will be an asset to you while cooking the recipes in this book.

Now, as I expand DinnerPlus with my first cookbook, and with so many other great things on the horizon, I can't help but be filled with joy and gratitude. Life has a funny way of moving us along. Whether with resistance or cooperation, we always end up where we are supposed to be. I'm beyond grateful to share this collection of recipes. Some of them have been updated from the versions you've seen on Instagram and TikTok, while others are the same. *Tastemaker* will serve as your essential handbook of recipes that will wow your guests. Whether it be a dinner for two or a group of six, *Tastemaker* has you covered.

My only request is that while reading this book and experiencing these recipes, you enjoy the journey of getting the meal to the table. Cooking is often approached as a daunting process, or something that needs to be quick and rushed. I, however, want you to make this a fun experience. Pour yourself a glass of wine, make a fab cocktail, turn on some good background music, and let trying my recipes be an enjoyable experience.

STAY READY

The most important thing while cooking and entertaining is preparation. Staying ready eliminates haste. My grandmother always said, "Haste makes waste, take your time."

Before cooking anything—whether large or small—I prepare. Getting everything chopped up, measured out, and organized keeps an even flow in the kitchen. Cleaning as you cook is very important, but the most important thing is having a clean, empty sink before cooking. No matter what you're making, you will need full access to the sink (even if just to wash your hands).

Another key component of staying ready is having a well-stocked pantry and kitchen. Here are a few of my must-have items in the kitchen.

PANTRY STAPLES

Apple cider vinegar

Assorted beans (chickpeas and dark-red kidney beans are a must for me)

Capers

Sriracha

Sun-dried tomatoes

Vanilla extract

GOOD FATS

Ghee (great for when you run out of butter)

Good-quality olive oil

High-temperature oil, such as avocado oil

Pure Irish salted butter (Kerrygold is my go-to)

FLAVOR ENHANCERS

Curry powder (I prefer Betapac)

Brown sugar

Dijon mustard

DinnerPlus spices (you'll really need them!)

Jamaican soup mix (I prefer Grace Cock)

Homemade stock (pages 158-159)

Honey

Light and dark soy sauce

Maggi

Chicken bouillon powder (I prefer Maggi)

Maldon sea salt

Kosher Salt (I prefer Diamond Crystal)

Mayonnaise

Walkerswood jerk seasoning

Whole and ground allspice

FRESH GOODS

Fresh herbs, especially thyme, rosemary, and parsley

Garlic (six to six hundred cloves of garlic!)

Ginger

Green onions

Lemons

Limes

Onions (all colors)

Parmesan cheese

Roma tomatoes

Spinach

STORAGE

Deli containers (great for storing stocks, residual oil, jus, sauces, and gravy)

Zip-top bags

Mason jars

TASTEMAKER TIP: *Measuring with your heart is always okay! The heart often knows that you can never have too much grated Parmesan or garlic, for instance. My heart certainly knows this when it comes to coarse black pepper and pinches of flaky sea salt!*

Cajunspice
savory smoke

oh.
——
wow.
——

DinnerPlus Spice
by Scot Louie

NET WT 7.1 OZ (204

OH, WOW SPICE SUBSTITUTIONS

Many of the recipes you'll find in this book were developed with my signature line of DinnerPlus spices. I highly recommend adding the complete collection to your pantry to experience that perfect balance of flavor, but the substitutions below will also work just fine. For any given recipe, if you don't have the DinnerPlus spices on hand, refer to this page to complete your dish.

To make each spice substitute, add 1 tablespoon of each ingredient listed and blend together until combined. Store in an airtight jar or container at room temperature for up to one month.

BRINING BLEND SUBSTITUTE

Himalayan Salt

Ground peppercorns

Thyme

Garlic powder

Onion powder

Lemon zest

Orange zest

Ground bay leaf

Ground sage

CAJUNSPICE SUBSTITUTE

Salt

Onion powder

Garlic powder

Smoked paprika

Black pepper

Cayenne pepper

Thyme

Oregano

Parsley

YARDSPICE SUBSTITUTE

Salt

Brown sugar

Paprika

Black pepper

Allspice

Cumin

Chili Flakes

Ginger

Thyme

ZESTYSPICE SUBSTITUTE

Salt

Garlic powder

Black pepper

Lemon zest

White pepper

Lemon juice

WHITESPICE SUBSTITUTE

Salt

Onion powder

Garlic powder

White pepper

Parsley

Canola Oil

Cocktails

BRUNCH PUNCH   17

SMOKE & BERRY   18

SORREL MARGARITA   21

PALOMA-ANN   22

BASIL SPRITZ   23

JAMAICAN RUM PUNCH   25

TAMARIND MARGARITA   26

ISLAND TING   28

YARD TODDY   29

TEA-TINI   30

BRUNCH PUNCH

MAKES 4–6 SERVINGS

16 oz blanco tequila

16 oz orange-pineapple juice

8 oz unfiltered apple juice

16 oz blood orange kombucha

Mint leaves for garnish

Orange slices for garnish

This recipe was birthed simply because I wanted something other than a mimosa with my brunch. I love a good mimosa, but they can get a bit repetitive. This vibrant punch is perfect for hosting, and, with a couple of kombuchas on hand, it made me feel a little less guilty about having tequila at 10 a.m. while not being on vacation.

Fill a large pitcher with ice. Add the tequila, orange-pineapple juice, and apple juice. Stir to combine.

Top up the pitcher with the kombucha and stir until combined. Pour into your desired glass and garnish with the mint leaves and orange slices.

SMOKE & BERRY

MAKES 2 COCKTAILS

1 cup fresh cranberries

4 oz mezcal

3 oz grenadine

2–3 dashes orange bitters

Club soda for topping

On my last trip to Mexico, I spent my twenty-seventh birthday at the RoMarley Beach House. Upon arrival, we were gifted many items, one of them being flasks of mezcal. If I could be any alcohol, I'd be mezcal. I love how smoky and sweet it is—much like me and this delicious cocktail.

Place the cranberries in a cocktail shaker and muddle them for about 2 minutes, until you have a pulp-like consistency.

Add the mezcal to the shaker and muddle the cranberries for another 1–2 minutes to ensure the mezcal soaks up the tangy flavor of the cranberries.

Add the grenadine and fill the shaker with ice. Cover and shake. Double strain the mixture into a short glass filled with ice.

Add the bitters, then gently mix. Top with club soda and enjoy!

SORREL MARGARITA

MAKES 4–6 SERVINGS

8 cups water

2 cups dried hibiscus flower

1 cup packed brown sugar

3-inch piece fresh ginger, peeled and chopped

10 allspice berries

6 whole cloves

Juice of 1 lime

2 oz tequila

1 oz simple syrup

Sorrel is a tangy, sweet, spice-infused drink that is often served during celebrations and holidays in Jamaica. I don't like sorrel, never did, even as a kid—I know, my Caribbean ancestors are weeping. I like to think I have made it up to them by concocting, and loving, this margarita. I recommend using a nice reposado tequila for this cocktail, but any will do.

To make the sorrel, in a large pot over medium-high heat, combine the water, hibiscus flower, brown sugar, ginger, allspice, and cloves and bring to a boil. Let boil, stirring occasionally, for about 8–10 minutes, until the color resembles that of the hibiscus flower and the hibiscus flower softens.

Remove the mixture from the heat and allow to steep at room temperature for at least 8 hours, and overnight if you can.

Once cooled, strain through a fine mesh strainer into a pitcher fitted with a lid. Store in the refrigerator for up to 3 days.

Fill a cocktail shaker with ice. Add the lime juice, tequila, 1 cup of sorrel, and the simple syrup. Shake well and pour into a glass filled with ice.

PALOMA-ANN

MAKES 1 COCKTAIL

2 tablespoons honey

3 fresh thyme sprigs

Juice of ½ large grapefruit

Juice of 1 lime

2 ice cubes

2 oz grapefruit-infused vodka, such as Absolut

Ting, or the grapefruit soda of your choice

This cocktail is something like the classic, but she's Jamaican (hence the "Ann"). The fresh thyme adds an herbaceous element that pairs perfectly with the citrus flavors of the grapefruit and lime. Miss Paloma-Ann is fizzy and, oh, so much fun. You can also make this recipe with your favorite tequila instead of vodka.

In a small saucepan over medium-low heat, combine the honey, thyme, grapefruit juice, and lime juice. Stir consistently for 3–5 minutes, until the mixture is combined and the thyme is fragrant. Remove from the heat. Add the ice cubes and mix well until cooled and combined. Set aside.

Fill a cocktail shaker fitted with a strainer with ice. Pour in the honey-citrus mixture and vodka. Shake well and strain into a glass filled with ice. Top with Ting and enjoy!

TASTEMAKER TIP: *You can also use prosecco, instead of Ting, for the fizzy topping in this drink.*

BASIL SPRITZ

MAKES 1 COCKTAIL

3–4 fresh basil leaves

1 tablespoon water

2 oz vodka

1½ oz yuzu liqueur

1 oz Ginger Simple Syrup
(page 143)

Prosecco for topping

I love a spritz—I'm all about anything that feels fresh, light, and bubbly! The taste that forms from the marriage of the basil and the yuzu is indescribable. You just have to try it. I am sure you'll understand after that first sip.

In a cocktail shaker fitted with a strainer, combine the basil and water, then muddle them until the basil is fragrant and broken down a bit.

Fill the cocktail shaker with ice, then add the vodka, yuzu liqueur, and simple syrup. Shake well, then pour the mixture into a glass filled with ice. Top with prosecco, mix slightly, and enjoy!

JAMAICAN RUM PUNCH

MAKES 4–6 SERVINGS

4 cups mango nectar

2¾ cups pineapple juice

2¾ cups orange juice

2 oz fresh lime juice
(about 2–4 limes)

8½ oz water

6 whole allspice berries

1-inch piece fresh ginger,
peeled

2 cups Wray & Nephew
white rum, or the brand of
your choice

8½ oz grenadine

8–10 dashes orange bitters

This sharable cocktail has the bold flavors of mango nectar, fresh ginger, and allspice. The mango nectar provides an unmatched richness, while the ginger and allspice add the perfect balance to cut through the sweetness and alcohol. Altogether, it makes a flavorful drink that is sure to be a crowd-pleaser.

In a large 1 gallon (128 oz) pitcher, combine the mango nectar, pineapple juice, orange juice, and lime juice.

In a blender, combine the water, allspice, and fresh ginger. Blend until smooth and no chunks are visible. Double strain through a cheesecloth over a fine mesh strainer directly into the pitcher containing the juice mixture.

Add the rum, grenadine, and bitters. Mix together until smooth and well combined.

Add more rum or juice to taste and enjoy!

TAMARIND MARGARITA

MAKES 1 COCKTAIL

TAMARIND REDUCTION

10 tamarind pods

Warm water for soaking

—

2 oz blanco tequila

1 oz tamarind reduction
(recipe at right)

1 oz Ginger Simple Syrup
(page 143)

1 oz fresh lime juice

Developing this cocktail was such a fun experience. If there's anything you try from this book, let it be this! As a child of the islands, I've always loved tamarind balls. They're candy rolled in sugar. You suck on them until you get past the sugar coating to the sticky, jammy nectar and then finally down to the seed. This margarita is tangy, sweet, and refreshing.

TAMARIND REDUCTION

Remove the tamarind from the pods and place them in a large bowl. Cover them with warm water and soak for 15 minutes, until the water is a bit brown in color.

Pour the tamarind and water into a medium saucepan and place over high heat. Once the water comes to a boil, reduce the heat to medium-low, cover, and simmer for 15–20 minutes. Remove from the heat and allow the mixture to cool.

Strain the mixture into a deli container or mason jar, pressing on the pulp to squeeze out all the liquid. You should be left with a mixture that has a gravy-like consistency and the seeds should be visible. Let cool. Store leftover reduction in a mason jar or other airtight container in the refrigerator for up to one week.

In a cocktail shaker fitted with a strainer filled with ice, combine the tequila, tamarind reduction, simple syrup, and lime juice. Shake well.

Strain into a glass filled with ice and enjoy.

ISLAND TING

MAKES 1 COCKTAIL

8 oz Ting, or the grapefruit soda of your choice

2 oz Wray & Nephew white rum, or the brand of your choice

1 oz Ginger Simple Syrup (page 143)

2 dashes orange bitters

Club soda for topping

My Jamaican roots have conditioned me to love a lot of things, two of them being rum and Ting. Ting is known as the secret weapon for cocktails, thanks to its subtle sweetness and refreshing bubbly blend of sparkling water and grapefruit. This cocktail is spritz-y and delicious.

In a mixing glass with ice, combine the soda, rum, simple syrup, and orange bitters. Throughly stir and then strain over a glass filled with ice. Top with club soda and enjoy.

YARD TODDY

MAKES 1 COCKTAIL

8 oz hot water

3 whole allspice berries

1 oz Wray & Nephew white rum, or the brand of your choice

1 oz fresh lime juice

2 tablespoons honey

Jamaican people have a natural remedy for everything. As a kid, this remedy was sure to kick any cold and fever symptoms—problematic, I know. However, now as an adult, it's one of my favorite warm, wintertime cocktails. This is the perfect cocktail to add to the menu for holiday gatherings such as Thanksgiving or Christmas.

In a medium saucepan over medium-high heat, combine the water and allspice berries and bring to a rolling boil, then remove from the heat.

Pour the rum into a mug, followed by the lime juice and honey. Pour the hot water through a strainer into the mug.

Mix well and enjoy hot!

TEA-TINI

MAKES 4-6 SERVINGS

⅔ cup honey

5½ cups water, divided

2 allspice berries

½ teaspoon ground cinnamon

4 oz vodka, divided

—

5 cups water

2 black tea bags

¼ cup sugar

½ teaspoon finely grated lemon zest

1 lemon, cut into wedges

2 dashes aromatic bitters

This could potentially be the most controversial statement I ever make—but I find coffee disgusting. As a bona fide tea drinker, I felt compelled to combat the espresso martini craze with this Tea-Tini. It smells *incredible* and tastes even better. Go ahead and pretend it's as healing as cuddling up with your favorite cup of tea.

To make the honey liqueur, combine the honey, ½ cup of water, the allspice, and cinnamon in a medium saucepan over medium-high heat and bring to a boil, stirring occasionally until a syrup-like texture is formed. Let the mixture cool, then pour it into a mason jar. Add 2 oz of vodka and shake to mix well.

In a medium pot over medium-high heat, bring 5 cups of water to a boil, then remove from the heat. Steep the tea bags for 10 minutes, then remove and discard them. Cool the tea in the refrigerator.

On a plate or in a shallow dish big enough to fit the rim of a martini glass, mix the sugar and lemon zest until combined.

Starting with your desired number of martini glasses, rub the rim of each martini glass with a lemon wedge and dip the rim of each glass into the lemon-sugar mixture. Tap any excess sugar back onto the plate.

Fill a cocktail shaker with ice. Add 1 cup of cooled tea, the remaining 2 oz of vodka, 1½ oz of honey liqueur, and the bitters. Shake well and pour into the prepared martini glasses.

TASTEMAKER TIP: *Make the honey liqueur ahead of time. Allowing it to sit at least overnight deepens the flavor. I store it in the cabinet for a few months and use it with my tea on occasion. However, you can use it sooner once you have allowed it to cool.*

Breakfast
& Brunch

TOASTED BRIOCHE WITH CREAM CHEESE
& STRAWBERRY COMPOTE   35

BAKED EGG BREAD BOWL   36

CHICKPEA COOK-UP   38

BREAKFAST POCKETS   39

HONEY BUTTER CORNBREAD WAFFLE   41

CALLALOO & SALTFISH FRITTERS   42

BREAKFAST CASSEROLE   44

JAMMY EGGS & HONEY BUTTER TOAST   45

TOASTED BRIOCHE WITH CREAM CHEESE & STRAWBERRY COMPOTE

MAKES 2 SLICES

2 slices (1-inch thick) brioche

2 oz cream cheese, at room temperature

2 tablespoons Strawberry Compote (page 152)

This Toasted Brioche moment is great for the days you're craving something a little naughty for breakfast but don't have the time or strength for pancakes or waffles... for instance, after a night of drinking. We've all been there. This dish is simple, sweet, and ready in minutes.

Toast the brioche. I love to toast it in a dry cast-iron skillet over medium heat for about 1 minute on each side. Keep a close eye! Brioche contains a bit more butter and is generally softer than most breads, so it tends to burn easily.

Spread on the cream cheese, then top with the compote and enjoy!

BAKED EGG BREAD BOWL

MAKES 4 SERVINGS

4 large soft rolls, such as brioche or bolillos

1 cup baby spinach leaves

About 1 teaspoon WhiteSpice (substitution, page 13)

½ lb bulk breakfast sausage

4 large eggs

4 teaspoons heavy cream

Kosher salt and freshly ground black pepper

1 teaspoon fresh thyme leaves, chopped

Chopped fresh flat-leaf parsley for garnish

Sun-Dried Tomato Aioli (page 149) for serving

I love finding new ways to enjoy classic comfort foods. I created this dish as a reimagined breakfast sandwich. The rolls for this recipe should be unsliced, so not hamburger style. The right roll may be easier to find in the deli section of your supermarket than in the bread aisle.

Preheat the oven to 350°F (180°C). Line a baking sheet with parchment paper or a silicone mat.

Slice off the top of the rolls, then scoop out the centers to create a bowl with a ½-inch-thick bottom and sides. (You can reserve the excess bread to make bread crumbs.)

Arrange the bread bowls on the prepared baking sheet. Line the bottom and sides of each bread bowl with ¼ cup of spinach, pressing it firmly into the bottom and sides of the bowls. Sprinkle a pinch of WhiteSpice over the spinach in each bowl.

In a small skillet over medium-high heat, cook the sausage, breaking up the meat with a wooden spatula, until nicely browned, about 5 minutes.

Add a quarter of the cooked sausage to each bread bowl, pressing it firmly into an even layer. Crack an egg directly over the sausage in each bowl. Pour 1 teaspoon of heavy cream over each egg.

Season each egg with a pinch of WhiteSpice, salt, pepper, and thyme.

Bake until the eggs are cooked through to your liking, 20–25 minutes for medium or up to 30 minutes for a firmer yolk.

Garnish with parsley and serve with aioli.

TASTEMAKER TIP: *If using a bread like ciabatta or Italian rolls, get a paper towel very wet and lay it on the bread for 2 minutes to moisten it; this will help prevent the bread from drying out too quickly in the oven.*

CHICKPEA COOK-UP

MAKES 4 SERVINGS

2 tablespoons avocado oil

½ cup diced Roma tomatoes

½ cup diced yellow onion

¼ cup diced red bell pepper

¼ cup diced green bell pepper

3 tablespoons minced garlic

1 can (15½ oz) can chickpeas, drained and rinsed

½ cup Chicken Stock (page 159)

1 cup chopped baby spinach

¼ cup ketchup

1 teaspoon YardSpice (substitution, page 13)

1 teaspoon WhiteSpice (substitution, page 13)

During an exquisite experience in Puerto Morelos, Mexico, I dined at a restaurant that offered a very enjoyable chickpea breakfast scramble. It was served with spinach, avocado, and blistered cherry tomatoes. I ate it every morning for a week. This recipe is inspired by that delicious travel memory, and since I've returned, it's had a permanent space in my breakfast rotation.

In a large skillet over medium-high heat, heat the avocado oil. Add the tomatoes, onion, and red and green bell peppers and sauté for 2 minutes, until the vegetables are softened. Add the garlic and sauté for 1–2 minutes.

Add the chickpeas and sauté for 2 minutes more. Add the stock, spinach, and ketchup, mixing until evenly combined and the spinach begins to wilt.

Season with YardSpice and WhiteSpice. Serve hot and enjoy!

TASTEMAKER TIP: *Try this topped with an over-easy egg, crusty bread, and avocado—chef's kiss!*

BREAKFAST POCKETS

MAKES 4 POCKETS

4 large eggs

Salt and freshly ground black pepper

1 tablespoon butter

1 package (8 oz) Pillsbury Crescent Rolls™

1 cup shredded Italian cheese blend, plus more for sprinkling

½ lb pork breakfast sausage links, cooked

Everything bagel seasoning

These are essentially elevated hot pockets, with the same satisfying steamy, cheese pull as the ones we loved as kids, a buttery flaky crust, and the perfect amount of seasoning. These pockets are great to have for a leisurely meal at home or to make ahead for a grab-n-go breakfast on those super busy mornings.

Preheat the oven to 375°F (190°C).

In a small bowl, beat 1 of the eggs until smooth to create an egg wash. Set aside.

In a separate small bowl, beat the remaining 3 eggs and season to taste with salt and pepper.

In a medium skillet over medium-low heat, melt the butter, then pour in the seasoned, beaten eggs. Cook for 1 minute undisturbed, then use a rubber spatula to drag the eggs across the pan until they're fully cooked, 3–4 minutes longer. Immediately remove the eggs from the heat.

Roll out the crescent roll dough. The dough is perforated, but do not separate it into the triangles. Instead, separate it into 4 rectangles on the prepared baking sheet, then press the perforated lines of each rectangle to seal.

Place ¼ cup of shredded cheese on 1 long side of each rectangle. Add a scoop of scrambled eggs and a sausage link. Starting on the long edge, fold each piece of dough closed and seal. Brush with the egg wash. Sprinkle with shredded cheese and season to taste with everything bagel seasoning.

Bake for 8–9 minutes, until golden brown. Serve hot and enjoy.

HONEY BUTTER CORNBREAD WAFFLE

**MAKES 4–6 SERVINGS;
ABOUT 12 STANDARD-SIZE
WAFFLES**

1½ cups fine yellow cornmeal

1 cup all-purpose flour

2 tablespoons sugar

2 teaspoons baking powder

1 teaspoon baking soda

1 teaspoon kosher salt

¼ teaspoon freshly grated
nutmeg

½ cup unsalted butter, plus
2 tablespoons for serving

½ cup honey, plus
2 tablespoons for serving

1 cup buttermilk

2 large eggs

1 teaspoon pure vanilla extract

Cooking spray

When the craving for a good waffle hits, I've got you all the way covered. I'm a huge fan of honey butter anything, but honey butter cornbread has a special place in my heart. Now, a Honey Butter Cornbread Waffle? That's a gift directly from the heavens.

Preheat the oven to 200°F (95°C) and place a baking sheet on the center rack; this will keep the waffles warm while you make them.

In a large bowl, whisk together the cornmeal, flour, sugar, baking powder, baking soda, salt, and nutmeg.

In a medium microwave-safe bowl, melt ½ cup of butter in the microwave for 30 second intervals. Increase by 15 seconds until you have fully melted butter. You don't want the butter too hot at this step, as it may start to cook the eggs. Add ½ cup of honey and stir until well combined. Add the buttermilk, eggs, and vanilla and whisk to combine.

Add the buttermilk mixture to the cornmeal mixture and whisk until just evenly combined.

Preheat a standard waffle iron to medium according to the manufacturer's instructions. Grease lightly with cooking spray. Add enough batter to fill each waffle mold (about ⅓ cup per waffle) and cook until just golden brown, about 2 minutes; watch the first batch carefully and adjust the timing according to your waffle iron.

As you make the waffles, place them on the baking sheet in the oven to keep them warm. Repeat with the remaining batter.

To serve, in a microwave-safe bowl, melt the remaining 2 tablespoons of butter in the microwave for 30–45 seconds. Stir in the remaining 2 tablespoons of honey. Drizzle the mixture over each waffle. Serve hot and enjoy!

TASTEMAKER TIP: *You can also make these into hot honey waffles by adding red pepper flakes to the honey butter mixture that you drizzle on top.*

CALLALOO & SALTFISH FRITTERS

MAKES 12 FRITTERS

10 oz salted pollock fillets

5 tablespoons coconut oil, divided

1 cup finely diced red bell peppers

1 cup finely diced green bell peppers

½ cup green onions, sliced

¼ cup yellow onion, finely diced

4 cloves garlic, minced

1 can (19 oz/540 g) callaloo, drained

3 fresh thyme sprigs

2 teaspoons YardSpice, divided (substitution, page 13)

1 cup all-purpose flour

1 teaspoon salt

½ teaspoon freshly ground black pepper

1 cup lukewarm water

Fritters have always been one of my favorite Jamaican breakfast foods. Traditionally, fritters are made with only saltfish, assorted sweet and hot peppers, and aromatics. I love challenging tradition, so I made fritters that use callaloo and saltfish. Callaloo is a leafy vegetable, similar to spinach, that is extremely popular in Caribbean countries.

Rinse the fish under warm water. Place the fish in a medium saucepan over medium-high heat, cover with water, and bring to a boil. Pour off the water and add fresh water. Bring to a boil again and repeat this process 2–3 times.

Drain the fish and flake it by hand.

Heat 2 tablespoons of coconut oil in a large skillet over medium-high heat. Add the red and green bell peppers, green onions, yellow onion, and garlic and sauté for 2 minutes, stirring constantly, until softened and fragrant.

Add the callaloo and flaked fish. Mix well to combine.

Add the thyme and 1 teaspoon of YardSpice. Mix well and remove from the heat.

Sift the flour into a large bowl. Season the flour with the remaining 1 teaspoon of YardSpice, the salt, and pepper.

Slowly whisk in the lukewarm water until a batter-like consistency is formed. Fold in the cooked callaloo mixture until evenly combined.

In a large skillet over medium heat, warm the remaining 3 tablespoons of coconut oil.

Using a ¼-cup measure, scoop out the batter and gently pour it into the skillet. Leave about 1 inch of space between the fritters.

Fry the fritters for 2–3 minutes, until the edges are golden. Gently flip and cook for 2 minutes longer on the opposite side. After flipping, gently press down the middle with the spatula to ensure the center cooks through.

Transfer the fritters to a plate lined with paper towels or a baking sheet with a wire rack to drain off the excess oil.

Serve hot and enjoy. Store any leftovers in an airtight container in the refrigerator for up to 3 days.

BREAKFAST CASSEROLE

MAKES 8–10 SERVINGS

Cooking spray

6 store-bought hash brown patties

8 large eggs

1 cup heavy cream

1 teaspoon salt

1 teaspoon freshly ground black pepper

½ lb bacon, chopped

1 lb ground breakfast sausage

4 cups shredded sharp Cheddar cheese

5 cups lightly packed baby spinach

This dish was birthed from a tale as old as time: a host running behind. I was hosting a brunch with friends and running terribly late in putting myself together. So, instead of making four separate dishes—hash browns, spinach and cheese eggs, bacon, and sausage—I made this delicious casserole that saved time without forfeiting flavor.

Preheat the oven to 375°F (190°C). Lightly grease a 9 x 13-inch baking dish with cooking spray.

Arrange the hash browns in the prepared dish, covering the bottom. Bake for 15 minutes, until noticeably defrosted.

Meanwhile, in a large mixing bowl, whisk together the eggs and heavy cream. Season with the salt and pepper. Set aside.

In a large frying pan over medium heat, cook the bacon until crisp, about 8–10 minutes, and set aside to cool. Chop the cooled bacon into bite-size pieces.

In the same pan over medium heat, cook the sausage in the bacon grease until browned, about 8–10 minutes. Set aside.

Remove the hash browns from the oven when done but keep the oven on. Immediately add about half of the cheese in a layer. Then add the spinach. Top the spinach with the cooked bacon and sausage. Pour the beaten eggs over everything, then top with the remaining cheese.

Cover tightly with aluminum foil and return the dish to the oven and bake for 30–40 minutes, until the cheese is fully melted and the eggs are firm. Remove the foil and bake uncovered for 5–8 minutes longer, until the cheese is bubbly and golden.

Serve hot and enjoy!

JAMMY EGGS & HONEY BUTTER TOAST

MAKES 2 SERVINGS

1 tablespoon white vinegar

Avocado oil spray

2 slices bread of choice

Butter

Honey

Salt and freshly ground
black pepper

This may seem like a quick breakfast, and, yes, it is. However, patience is still required. Jammy eggs are a work of art and require some finesse to get the perfect consistency. Take your time with this one and prepare to savor the result.

Bring a medium saucepan of water to a boil over high heat, then add the vinegar. Use a slotted spoon to gently lower the eggs into the water. Reduce the heat to medium to maintain a gentle boil. Cook the eggs for 7 minutes and 7 seconds (the 7 seconds are for good luck).

While the eggs cook, prepare an ice bath (ice and water) in a small bowl. When the cooking time is up, immediately transfer the eggs to the ice bath to stop the cooking process. Let them cool for 3–4 minutes, then peel and halve them.

Lightly grease a medium skillet with avocado oil spray and place it over medium-high heat. Add the bread slices and toast them for 2–3 minutes per side, until golden brown.

Butter the toast immediately and drizzle with honey. Top with the jammy eggs, add a pinch of salt and pepper, and enjoy!

Appetizers & All-Day Meals

CHORIZO TACO CUPS 49

GARLIC LEMON PEPPER WINGS 50

JERK CHICKEN BURRITO 52

MASON JAR NOODLE SOUP 53

BOUGIE CHOPPED CHEESE SLIDERS 55

STICKY FRIED SHORT RIBS 56

CAESAR TOAST 57

CARMELIZED SHALLOT & ROASTED GARLIC LOBSTER BISQUE 59

HOT HONEY CRISPY SHRIMP 60

ELEVATED SNACK WRAPS 62

MUSTARD CHICKEN BITES 63

CRAB RANGOON DIP 65

CHORIZO TACO CUPS

**MAKES 12 SERVINGS;
12 TACO CUPS**

1 lb ground chorizo

4 fresh cilantro sprigs,
chopped

1 small yellow onion, diced

2 teaspoons tomato bouillon
powder

1 teaspoon CajunSpice
(substitution, page 13)

½ teaspoon sugar

1 package (12 count) soft
street taco tortillas, such as
Mission

1½ cups shredded Mexican
blend cheese (optional)

These customizable taco cups make the perfect snack or appetizer
for guests. I recommend setting up a topping station when
serving these. Offer olives, shredded lettuce, refried beans, cotija
cheese, guacamole, pico de gallo, sour cream—the possibilities are
endless! It's a great way to gather around a bar top or table and get
the conversation flowing.

Preheat the oven to 350°F (180°C).

Place the chorizo in a dry, medium skillet over medium heat. Cook, using a
spatula to break up the chorizo and stirring occasionally, for 5–7 minutes,
until browned and crumbly. Drain off any excess fat and oil.

In the same pan, still over medium heat, add the cilantro, onion, tomato
bouillon powder, CajunSpice, and sugar. Cook, stirring occasionally, for
3–4 minutes, until the onions are softened and everything is well
combined. Remove from the heat and set aside.

Halve the tortillas and moisten them with a little water to ensure they don't
dry out in the oven. In an ungreased and unlined muffin pan, place 2 tortilla
halves in each cup, laying them in opposite directions.

Using the back of a spoon, gently press the center and sides of tortillas
together—they should take on the shape of the muffin cup.

Fill each taco cup with a bit of the cooked chorizo mixture and a sprinkle of
cheese (if using). Bake for 8–12 minutes, until the shells are golden brown
at the tips and the cheese is completely melted.

Enjoy with your favorite toppings.

TASTEMAKER TIP: *My go-to toppings are pico de gallo, sour cream,
lettuce, a smidge of taco sauce, and jalapeños... in that order!*

GARLIC LEMON PEPPER WINGS

**MAKES 4 SERVINGS;
16–20 WINGS**

2 lb party chicken wings

Vinegar for cleaning wings

1 cup DinnerPlus Brining
Blend

2 tablespoons avocado oil

2 tablespoons ZestySpice
(substitution, page 13)

1 teaspoon WhiteSpice
(substitution, page 13)

1 teaspoon CajunSpice
(substitution, page 13)

½ teaspoon salt

Whether it's for a chic cocktail party or game day gathering, you can't go wrong with a classic chicken wing moment. These Garlic Lemon Pepper Wings add a little flare and pack lots of flavors in each bite. I often opt for a dry rub for less breading. Be sure to serve with a range of assorted dipping sauces.

Preheat the oven to 400°F (200°C). Line a baking sheet with parchment paper.

Prepare and clean your wings. In a large bowl, coat and toss the wings in vinegar and rinse them under warm running water, filling and draining the bowl 3–4 times.

Bring a large pot of water to a boil over high heat, then add the Brining Blend. Stir to dissolve and reduce the heat to medium. Add the washed chicken wings and cook, stirring occasionally and ensuring the water doesn't return to a boil, for 4–5 minutes, until the skin of the chicken begins to tighten and firm.

Drain the wings and pat them dry with a paper towel.

Transfer the wings to a large bowl. Add avocado oil and toss to coat, then add the ZestySpice, WhiteSpice, CajunSpice, and salt, tossing to coat.

Arrange the wings on the prepared baking sheet. Bake for 45 minutes, flipping the wings halfway through, until golden and slightly crispy. Serve hot.

JERK CHICKEN BURRITO

MAKES 1 SERVING; 1 BURRITO

¼ cup corn, drained and rinsed

¼ cup diced Roma tomatoes

1 small shallot, finely diced

Juice of ½ lime (about 2 teaspoons)

1 (10-inch) tortilla

⅓ cup shredded Cheddar cheese

⅓ cup cooked jerk chicken, cubed

¼ cup Jamaican Rice & "Peas" (page 77)

¼ cup shredded cabbage

1 tablespoon butter

2 teaspoons Scotch Bonnet Aioli (page 151)

I like to think of this dish as the tasty result of two cultures colliding. A Mexican cuisine staple, the burrito, meets a Jamaican cuisine staple, jerk chicken. Paired with rice, cheese, veggies, and wrapped in a golden tortilla, this Jerk Chicken Burrito is the perfect union of delicious flavors.

In a small bowl, combine the corn, tomatoes, shallot, and lime juice. Mix well and set aside.

Place the tortilla on a clean surface. I find its easier to wrap when the ingredients are laid out in thin layers below the center of the tortilla. Start by adding the cheese, then add the chicken, rice and peas, ¼ cup of corn-tomato mixture, and the cabbage.

Before folding the burrito, start melting the butter in a large skillet over medium-low heat.

Fold the 2 outer sides of the tortilla inward. Then fold the bottom (closer to the filling) to cover the filling. Roll the rest of the way as tightly as you can (without tearing the tortilla).

With the seam-side down, gently place the burrito in the melted butter. Raise the heat to medium high. Cook for 2 minutes per side, until golden brown.

Remove from the heat and enjoy while hot.

TASTEMAKER TIP: *Rinsing the shallot under cold water reduces the chance of lingering aroma after enjoying this meal.*

MASON JAR NOODLE SOUP

**MAKES 2 SERVINGS;
1 X 24 OZ JAR OF SOUP**

2 cups water

3 tablespoons sweet white miso paste

1 teaspoon chicken bouillon powder

1 teaspoon chili crisp in oil

1 teaspoon light soy sauce

1 package (6 oz) cooked instant noodles (from the refrigerated section of the grocery store)

½ cup lightly packed baby spinach

¼ cup sliced green onion

½ cup cubed medium-firm tofu

1 teaspoon sesame oil (optional)

For those who work a 9–5 and are all out of ideas on what to bring for lunch at the office, look no further. These noodles are the perfect lunch to prep ahead and finish making when you're ready to eat, wherever you are. This soup is warm, flavorful, and filling—the perfect combination to give you a boost to make it through that workday.

Place the water in a medium kettle or saucepan and bring to a boil over medium-high heat.

While the water boils, put the miso paste in a 24-oz mason jar. Add the chicken bouillon powder, chili crisp, and soy sauce. I like to whisk those together, so the mixture dissolves easier, but this step is optional.

Rinse the instant noodles under cold water, then add them to the jar. Add the spinach, green onion, and tofu.

Pour the boiling water into the jar. Using chopsticks, gently mix everything together, loosening up the noodles and bringing the flavor up from the bottom.

Top with sesame oil (if using). Allow 2–3 minutes of steeping time. Enjoy!

BOUGIE CHOPPED CHEESE SLIDERS

**MAKES 6 SERVINGS;
12 SLIDERS**

1 lb ground Kobe beef patties

2 teaspoons sazón seasoning

1 teaspoon adobo seasoning

2 teaspoons WhiteSpice,
divided (substitution, page 13)

1 teaspoon salt

1 teaspoon freshly ground
black pepper

1 shallot, finely diced

1 package (8 oz) creamy
Havarti cheese, sliced

2 tablespoons butter

1 package (12 count) slider
buns, such as King's Hawaiian

Shredded iceberg lettuce
for topping

1 Roma tomato, cut into
12 slices

Chipotle Sauce (page 155)
for topping

Before I'm anything else, I'm a New Yorker—a Brooklyn New Yorker. I grew up loving my local corner store/deli where chopped cheese sliders are the holy grail. Lately, there's been a debate about which borough makes the best chopped cheese... well, pass the crown because it'll be you after you make these sliders.

Preheat the oven to 350°F (180°C).

In a large skillet over medium-high heat, cook the beef for 3 minutes, using a spatula to break the meat down.

Season with the sazón, adobo, 1 teaspoon of WhiteSpice, salt, and pepper. Add the shallot and continue cooking until the meat is fully browned and the shallot is softened, about 3–4 minutes.

Add the Havarti and stir until melted and combined. Remove from the heat.

In a small microwave-safe bowl, melt the butter in the microwave for 30–45 seconds, until softened. Add the remaining 1 teaspoon of WhiteSpice, mixing to combine.

With a bread knife, halve each bun widthwise, creating a top and bottom slice. Using a pastry brush, coat the top of each bun with some of the butter mixture. Place the buns, open faced, onto a 9 x 13-inch baking sheet. Add the cooked beef mixture to the bottom half of each bun and bake for 8–10 minutes.

Remove the pan from the oven and top each slider with the lettuce and tomato. Add a dollop of chipotle sauce to the inside of each top bun and assemble. Brush the buns with the remaining butter mixture. Serve hot and enjoy!

STICKY FRIED SHORT RIBS

MAKES 4–6 SERVINGS

2 lb flank-style beef short ribs

1 tablespoon white vinegar

2 tablespoons cornstarch

2 teaspoons baking soda

2 tablespoons soy sauce

1 tablespoon oyster sauce

1 tablespoon dark brown sugar

6 cloves garlic, grated

1-inch piece fresh ginger, peeled and grated

1 teaspoon WhiteSpice (substitution, page 13)

1 teaspoon YardSpice (substitution, page 13)

Vegetable oil for frying

2–3 teaspoons honey

Toasted sesame seeds for garnish

These Fried Short Ribs have been a starter staple at many of my dinner parties over the years, so I like to think they have been practiced to perfection. The baking soda helps tenderize the beef, but it needs to be marinated for a few hours to activate.

Cut the ribs crosswise between each bone. Transfer to a large bowl, cover with cold water, and add the vinegar. Set aside for 30 minutes. Drain and pat dry.

Wipe out the bowl, then add the cornstarch and baking soda. Whisk together until well combined. Add the soy sauce, oyster sauce, brown sugar, garlic, ginger, WhiteSpice, and YardSpice and stir until well combined. Add the rib pieces and gently toss until they are evenly coated with the paste. Cover and refrigerate for at least 2 hours or up to overnight.

Fill a large saucepan with about 2 inches of oil (do not fill it more than half full). Heat the oil over medium-high heat until a deep-frying thermometer registers 350°F (180°C).

Working in batches to avoid overcrowding, fry the short rib pieces, turning once or twice with tongs, until nicely browned and cooked through, about 3 minutes. Transfer to paper towels or a wire rack to drain. Repeat for all the pieces, making sure to let the oil come back up to temperature between batches.

Arrange the ribs on a platter, drizzle with honey, and garnish with sesame seeds. Serve at once.

CAESAR TOAST

MAKES ABOUT 6 SERVINGS

1 large head romaine lettuce, chopped

Roasted Garlic Caesar Dressing (page 147)

1 ciabatta or baguette, cut into 1-inch slices (10–12 pieces)

1 tablespoon olive oil

2 tablespoons grated Parmesan cheese

Maldon sea salt and freshly ground black pepper

An excellent party starter! These crunchy delights are classy, yet simple, and perfect for the days you'd like a healthy option. You can always get festive and dress them up even more with your favorite veggies or meat. Sometimes I like to add a dollop of seafood salad or grilled shrimp to top each slice.

Preheat the oven to 350°F (180°C). Line a baking sheet with aluminum foil.

In a large bowl, combine the romaine and dressing, tossing to coat evenly. Place in the refrigerator.

Meanwhile, arrange the ciabatta or baguette slices on a baking sheet. Drizzle each slice with the olive oil, then sprinkle with the Parmesan and season to taste with salt and pepper.

Bake on 350°F (180°C) for 10–12 minutes, until nicely toasted and golden.

Remove from the oven and allow 2–3 minutes to cool.

Once cooled, place the ciabatta or baguette slices on your desired serving platter and top with the Caesar salad mixture. Enjoy!

CARAMELIZED SHALLOT & ROASTED GARLIC LOBSTER BISQUE

MAKES 4 SERVINGS

FOR THE CARAMELIZED SHALLOTS

8 tablespoons butter

3 tablespoons olive oil

1 lb shallots, sliced

FOR THE BISQUE

4 tablespoons butter

1 tablespoon olive oil

4 ribs celery, chopped

2 large carrots, chopped

1 large white onion, diced

3 fresh thyme sprigs

1 teaspoon chopped fresh tarragon

1 teaspoon chopped fresh flat-leaf parsley

1 head Perfect Roasted Garlic (page 150)

2 teaspoons salt

1 teaspoon freshly ground black pepper

4 tablespoons tomato paste

¼ cup all-purpose flour

2 cups white wine

6 cups Seafood Stock (page 158)

2 teaspoons Old Bay Seasoning

1 teaspoon WhiteSpice (substitution, page 13)

1 teaspoon CajunSpice (substitution, page 13)

2 bay leaves

4 lobster tails (½ lb each), shelled and cubed

1 cup heavy cream

Minced chives for garnish

This bisque was a game changer for me when I first tasted it. The sweetness of the caramelized shallot combined with the sweet and nutty flavor of the roasted garlic takes this bisque to higher heights. Enjoy with a slice of toasted baguette or crunchy croutons.

To make the caramelized shallots, in large skillet over medium heat, melt the butter and olive oil. Add the shallots and sugar. Mix well. Cook, stirring occasionally, for 35–40 minutes, until the shallots are softened and caramel in color. Set aside.

To make the bisque, in a large pot over medium heat, melt the butter and olive oil. Add the celery, carrots, onion, thyme, tarragon, and parsley and cook, stirring occasionally, for 5–6 minutes, until the vegetables are softened. Add the caramelized shallots and roasted garlic, cooking for 1 minute longer. Season with the salt and black pepper.

Add the tomato paste and flour and cook for 2–3 minutes. The consistency should be a bit chunky. Add the white wine, mixing the ingredients. Cook, stirring occasionally, until the wine is reduced by half, about 3–4 minutes.

Add the stock, Old Bay, WhiteSpice, CajunSpice, and bay leaves. Mix well and reduce the heat to medium-low, allowing the ingredients to simmer for 25 minutes.

Remove and discard the woody thyme stems and the bay leaves.

Turn off the heat and, using an immersion blender, blend the soup until smooth. Alternatively, use a blender; make sure to remove the steam valve and blend in batches.

Once the soup is smooth, return it to medium heat.

Add the cubed lobster meat. Cook for 5–6 minutes, until pink and opaque, then add the heavy cream, stirring to combine.

Garnish with chives and enjoy!

HOT HONEY CRISPY SHRIMP

MAKES 4 SERVINGS

1 lb large shrimp, peeled and deveined

4 teaspoons YardSpice, divided (substitution, page 13)

2 teaspoons CajunSpice, divided (substitution, page 13)

2 teaspoons WhiteSpice, divided (substitution, page 13)

2 teaspoons salt, divided, plus more to taste, beaten

½ cup panko bread crumbs

½ cup cornstarch

2 cups vegetable oil

4 tablespoons butter

1 teaspoon cayenne pepper

¼ cup hot sauce

¼ cup honey

Chopped fresh flat-leaf parsley or chives for serving

These Hot Honey Crispy Shrimp have quickly become a party favorite and a new brunch staple in my household. Shrimp are versatile and can be prepared and enjoyed many ways. This sweet and spicy combination has proven to be one of my favorite ways to dress them.

Place the shrimp in a large bowl, then season with 2 teaspoons of YardSpice, 1 teaspoon of CajunSpice, 1 teaspoon of WhiteSpice, and 1 teaspoon of salt.

Pour the beaten egg over the shrimp. Mix so all the shrimp are coated in egg. Rest for 15 minutes.

In a large zip-top bag, mix the bread crumbs, cornstarch, 1 teaspoon of YardSpice, the remaining 1 teaspoon of CajunSpice, and the remaining 1 teaspoon of WhiteSpice.

Add the shrimp to the bag and shake well, until they're all evenly coated in the bread crumb mixture. Transfer the shrimp to a wire rack or plate and let them rest 15–20 minutes longer.

In a large, deep skillet over medium heat, warm the vegetable oil until a deep-frying thermometer registers 350°F (180°C).

Working in batches, fry the shrimp for 2 minutes per side and then immediately transfer to paper towels to drain. Do not cook a moment longer or the shrimp will get rubbery.

Season immediately with a few pinches of salt.

In a small saucepan over medium-low heat, melt the butter with the remaining 1 teaspoon of YardSpice and the cayenne pepper, whisking occasionally. Add the hot sauce and honey, whisking occasionally until evenly combined and reduced to a sticky, saucy consistency, about 2–3 minutes.

Place the shrimp in a large bowl and pour the hot honey sauce over the top, tossing the shrimp gently until evenly coated. Top with parsley and serve at once.

ELEVATED SNACK WRAPS

MAKES 6 SERVINGS

FOR THE DIJONNAISE

½ cup mayonnaise

¼ cup Dijon mustard

3 tablespoons honey

1 tablespoon hot honey, such as Mike's Hot Honey

—

1 lb chicken breast, thinly sliced

1 teaspoon salt

1 teaspoon freshly ground black pepper

2 teaspoons WhiteSpice (substitution, page 13)

1 teaspoon ZestySpice (substitution, page 13)

1 teaspoon YardSpice (substitution, page 13)

1 teaspoon CajunSpice (substitution, page 13)

1 tablespoon avocado oil

3 (10-inch) tortillas, halved

Butter lettuce, shredded, for topping

Shredded Gruyère cheese for toppinge

I am not a huge fan of fast food, but if there is one fast food item I occasionally miss, it's the McDonald's snack wrap. This elevated version was in heavy rotation during the early days of my styling career, when I was always on the go and strapped for cash, and I still enjoy one to this day.

To make the Dijonnaise, in a small bowl with a lid, whisk together the mayonnaise, mustard, honey, and hot honey until smooth. Refrigerate until ready to use.

Place the chicken breast in a medium bowl with a lid. Season with the salt, black pepper, WhiteSpice, ZestySpice, YardSpice, and CajunSpice. Rub the seasonings to coat the chicken and let marinate at room temperature for 30–60 minutes.

In a large skillet over medium heat, warm the avocado oil. Add the chicken pieces and cook on both sides for 3–4 minutes, until golden. Remove from the heat and rest.

To assemble with wraps, set out the tortilla halves. Spread about 1 teaspoon of Dijonnaise on each half, then top with lettuce, cooked chicken, and cheese. Roll up the tortillas from end to end and secure them with a toothpick before serving.

MUSTARD CHICKEN BITES

MAKES 6 SERVINGS

1 lb chicken breast, cut into 1-inch pieces

½ cup buttermilk

¼ cup yellow mustard

1 tablespoon ground mustard

1 tablespoon confectioners' sugar

1 tablespoon salt

2 teaspoons CajunSpice (substitution, page 13)

2 teaspoons WhiteSpice (substitution, page 13)

FOR THE DREDGE

2 cups all-purpose flour

½ cup confectioners' sugar

2 tablespoons ground mustard

1 tablespoon salt

1 teaspoon CajunSpice

1 teaspoon WhiteSpice

—

Canola oil for frying

Dijonnaise (page 62) for serving

Another remixed fast-food craving, with more freshness and flavor than you'll find in any drive-through. The tangy mustard and juicy, well-seasoned chicken make these breaded bites an addicting and delectable appetizer for your guests, or an anytime snack for yourself. I recommend enjoying with the Dijonnaise (page 62) but try them with any of your favorite dipping sauces.

Place the chicken in a medium bowl with a lid. Pour the buttermilk over the chicken, then add the yellow mustard. Season with the ground mustard, sugar, salt, CajunSpice, and WhiteSpice. Cover and let the chicken marinate for at least 30 minutes in the refrigerator, or up to overnight.

Remove the chicken 30–60 minutes before you want to dredge.

To make the dredge, in a large bowl, whisk together the flour, sugar, ground mustard, salt, CajunSpice, and WhiteSpice until evenly combined.

Dredge the chicken in the flour mixture, tapping off any excess flour. Repeat until all the chicken is coated with the mixture. Rest the pieces on a clean baking sheet or wire rack for 10–15 minutes before frying.

In a large, deep skillet over medium heat, warm about 2 inches of oil until a deep-frying thermometer registers 350°F (180°C). Working in batches, add the chicken and fry for 3–4 minutes, or until golden brown. Transfer to a wire rack to drain.

Serve with Dijonnaise and enjoy.

CRAB RANGOON DIP

MAKES 4–6 SERVINGS

3 cups chopped imitation crabmeat

1 package (8 oz) cream cheese, at room temperature

1½ cups Kewpie mayo

2 green onions, sliced into thin rounds

1 teaspoon ground white pepper

½ cup shredded mozzarella cheese

2 cloves garlic, grated

Pita or wonton chips for serving

With Chinese takeout being a New York staple, I adore a classic, crispy Crab Rangoon. As someone who loves to entertain and loves to save time even more, making this dip was the perfect balance of both. This dip is the ideal shareable appetizer and much more convenient than preparing twenty-five individual Crab Rangoons.

Preheat the oven to 400°F (200°C).

In a medium bowl, mix the crabmeat, cream cheese, Kewpie mayo, green onions, and white pepper. Transfer the crab mixture to an ungreased 8 x 12-inch baking dish or to two 4-inch-square ramekins on top of a baking sheet. Top with the cheese.

Bake for 12–15 minutes, until bubbly. Preheat the broiler and broil for 3–4 minutes, until the cheese is bubbly and golden brown.

Serve hot with pita chips and enjoy.

DinnerPlus

OVEN JERK CHICKEN 68

SAUSAGE & SUN-DRIED TOMATO
STUFFED SHELLS 71

CREAMY SCALLOP PAPPARDELLE 73

JERK MAC & CHEESE WITH CREAMY JERK SAUCE 75

JAMAICAN RICE & "PEAS" 77

SWEET SAUSAGE SMASH BURGER 78

JAMAICAN OXTAIL 81

BROWN STEW CHICKEN 83

CHICKEN MEATBALLS WITH GARLIC
BUTTER SAUCE & ORZO SALAD 84

ONE-PAN MAPLE CHICKEN & RICE 85

JUMP-START CHICKEN 87

RASTA RISOTTO 88

BROWN BUTTER TORTELLINI 89

GOCHUJANG CRAB NOODLES 90

BBL FRIED CABBAGE 93

THREE SAUCE NAAN PIZZA WITH CRISPY PROSCIUTTO 95

TURMERIC-GINGER BRANZINO 96

GARLICKY LEMON PEPPER LAMB CHOPS
WITH HONEY GLAZE 99

SOUL BOWL SERIES 100

OVEN JERK CHICKEN

MAKES 4–6 SERVINGS

2 lb chicken leg quarters, washed

1 tablespoon olive oil

½ cup Jamaican Green Seasoning (page 156)

1 tablespoon dry jerk seasoning, such as Easispice

1 tablespoon jerk seasoning, such as Walkerswood

1 tablespoon dark brown sugar

2 teaspoons YardSpice (substitution, page 13)

2 teaspoons CajunSpice (substitution, page 13)

2 teaspoons salt

We've made it to the star of the show. As a Jamaican, I view learning to prepare jerk chicken properly as a rite of passage. Traditionally, jerk chicken is made outdoors over pimento wood, but this is one of the first dishes I learned to perfect in an oven. Oven Jerk Chicken is a pure heaven of flavor and spice.

Place the chicken in a large bowl or zip-top bag. Add the olive oil, green seasoning, dry jerk seasoning, jerk seasoning, brown sugar, YardSpice, CajunSpice, and salt. Rub the seasonings over the chicken well, ensuring that you get under the skin. I like to poke little slits in the chicken with a knife to ensure deeper marinating. Refrigerate for 24–36 hours.

Remove the chicken from the refrigerator 30–45 minutes before you want to cook it.

Preheat the oven to 400°F (200°C). Line a baking sheet with aluminum foil and place a roasting rack on top.

Arrange the marinated chicken on the prepared rack and brush on any leftover marinade.

Bake for 15 minutes, then reduce the oven temperature to 350°F (180°C) and bake for 50–60 minutes longer, until an instant-read thermometer inserted into the thickest part of the chicken registers 165°F (74°C).

Remove from the oven and rest for 10 minutes, uncovered, before serving.

SAUSAGE & SUN-DRIED TOMATO STUFFED SHELLS

MAKES 8 SERVINGS

FOR THE PASTA

1 box (12 oz) large pasta shells

Olive oil for drizzling

FOR THE SAUSAGE FILLING

1 lb sweet Italian sausage, casings removed

½ lb hot Italian sausage, casings removed

1 small shallot, finely chopped

1 teaspoon Italian seasoning

1 teaspoon kosher salt

1 teaspoon fennel seed

½ teaspoon sugar

FOR THE RICOTTA FILLING

1 lb (2 cups) whole-milk ricotta cheese

1 large egg

1 cup shredded mozzarella cheese

½ teaspoon kosher salt

½ teaspoon freshly ground black pepper

1 tablespoon minced fresh basil

I love to serve these stuffed shells with a vibrant side salad full of fresh veggies. This is a very rich dish, but so worth it. If you prefer to lighten it up a little, you can easily omit the cream sauce and top with 3–4 cups of store-bought marinara.

To make the pasta, bring a large pot of salted water to a rolling boil over high heat. Add the shells and cook, stirring occasionally, until just al dente, about 9 minutes. Drain, rinse under cold water, and drain again. Spread the cooked shells on a rimmed baking sheet and drizzle with olive oil. Toss to coat and set aside.

To make the sausage filling, place both types of sausage in a large skillet over medium-high heat. Cook, using a wooden spatula to break the sausage into fine pieces, until browned, about 7 minutes. Add the shallot and cook, stirring, until softened and fragrant, about 3 minutes. Stir in the Italian seasoning, salt, fennel seed, and sugar. Transfer the mixture to a medium bowl and wipe out the pan.

To make the ricotta filling, in a medium bowl, add the ricotta and egg and whisk to combine. Fold in the mozzarella, salt, pepper, and basil. Set aside.

To make the sauce, in the large skillet over medium heat, warm the olive oil. Add the sun-dried tomatoes and garlic and sauté until fragrant, 1–2 minutes. Pour in the half-and-half and reduce the heat to medium-low. Whisk in the pesto, Parmesan, parsley, WhiteSpice, and Italian seasoning. Season to taste with salt and pepper. Let the sauce simmer gently until slightly thickened, about 2 minutes.

Preheat the oven to 375°F (190°C). Grease a 9 x 13-inch baking dish with olive oil.

To assemble, stuff each shell with 1 heaping tablespoon of ricotta and 1 heaping tablespoon of the sausage mixture, dividing it evenly between the shells.

Continued on next page...

Recipe continued from previous page...

FOR THE SAUCE

1 tablespoon olive oil

¼ cup finely chopped sun-dried tomatoes in olive oil

3 cloves garlic, minced

2 cups half-and-half

½ cup sun-dried tomato pesto

⅓ cup grated Parmesan

2 tablespoons chopped fresh flat-leaf parsley

2 teaspoons WhiteSpice (substitution, page 13)

1 teaspoon Italian seasoning

Kosher salt and freshly ground black pepper

—

Olive oil for greasing

1½ cups shredded Italian cheese blend

Fresh basil, cut into ribbons, for garnish

Arrange the stuffed shells in the prepared baking dish; you will need to fit them very snugly and they will overlap. Top with the Italian cheese blend. Pour the sauce over all the shells. Cover the dish tightly with aluminum foil and bake until heated through and bubbling, 25–30 minutes.

Remove the foil and preheat the broiler with a rack about 6 inches from the heat source. Broil the shells until the top is nicely browned, about 3 minutes. Garnish with the basil. Serve hot and enjoy.

CREAMY SCALLOP PAPPARDELLE

MAKES 4 SERVINGS

5 quarts water

4 tablespoons plus 1 teaspoon salt, divided

1 package (16 oz) pappardelle pasta

1 lb sea scallops, rinsed

1½ teaspoons freshly ground black pepper, divided

½ tablespoon all-purpose flour

4 tablespoons butter, divided

1 tablespoon olive oil, plus more for the pasta

6 cloves garlic, minced

2 cups heavy cream

3 cups lightly packed baby spinach

3 teaspoons CajunSpice (substitution, page 13)

1 teaspoon WhiteSpice (substitution, page 13)

Grated Parmesan for serving

This recipe was featured in my very first viral video, racking up one million views in less than a week. So, in deciding which dinner recipes to share in this cookbook, she had to make the cut! A good pasta always stays in my meal rotation. This pasta is wonderfully creamy, without feeling too heavy.

In a large pot over medium-high heat, bring the water to a boil and add 4 tablespoons of salt. Add the pasta and cook until al dente, 6–8 minutes. Drain, coat with oil to prevent sticking, and set aside.

Rinse the scallops under tepid water. Lay them on a cutting board lined with paper towels. Using additional paper towels, pat the scallops dry.

Season the scallops with ½ teaspoon of salt and ½ teaspoon of pepper. Sprinkle the flour onto the tops of the scallops and allow them to rest for 5–6 minutes.

In a large skillet over medium heat, melt 2 tablespoons of butter with the olive oil. Add the scallops, floured side down, and cook for 2 minutes uninterrupted. Flip and cook for 1 minute longer, until browned. Set the scallops aside on a separate dish.

Add the remaining 2 tablespoons of butter to deglaze the pan, still over medium heat. Add the garlic and cook, stirring occasionally, for 1 minute, until fragrant.

Add the heavy cream and reduce the heat to medium-low. Add the spinach and season with the remaining ½ teaspoon of salt, remaining 1 teaspoon of pepper, the CajunSpice, and WhiteSpice.

Mix well and then add the cooked pasta, gently mixing until all the pasta is coated in the sauce.

Add parmesan as desired, then remove from the heat. Transfer the pasta mixture to a serving dish, top the with the scallops, add more grated parmesan, and serve.

JERK MAC & CHEESE WITH CREAMY JERK SAUCE

MAKES 6–8 SERVINGS

FOR THE JERK CHICKEN

2 tablespoons jerk seasoning, such as Walkerswood

1 tablespoon avocado oil

2 teaspoons YardSpice (substitution, page 13)

2 teaspoons WhiteSpice (substitution, page 13)

1 teaspoon kosher salt

1 teaspoon dark brown sugar

1 teaspoon chopped fresh thyme leaves

2 cloves garlic, minced

1 teaspoon peeled and finely grated fresh ginger

1 green onion, white and green parts finely chopped

1½ lb boneless skinless chicken thighs, cut into 1-inch pieces (about 6 thighs)

By now, you may have noticed my tendency to add jerk chicken to deliciously cheesy dishes. I truly believe jerk chicken is the gift that keeps on giving, and there are no rules when it comes to elevating a dish beyond tradition. This trio of cheesy mac, jerk chicken, and creamy jerk sauce may be my greatest combination yet.

To make the jerk chicken, in a medium bowl, whisk together the jerk seasoning, avocado oil, YardSpice, WhiteSpice, salt, brown sugar, thyme, garlic, ginger, and green onion. Add the chicken, mix well, and set aside to marinate for 20 minutes at room temperature, or up to 3 hours in the refrigerator.

To make the mac and cheese, in a large pot, combine the chicken broth, water, and salt. Bring to a boil over high heat. Add the macaroni and cook, stirring occasionally, until al dente, about 6 minutes or according to package instructions. Drain well and set aside.

In a medium bowl, combine the Gouda and Cheddar cheeses. Set aside.

Place the pot over medium heat and add the butter and garlic. When the butter is melted, whisk in the half-and-half, evaporated milk, CajunSpice, WhiteSpice, YardSpice, pepper, and jerk seasoning. Mix well until evenly combined. Add half (about 2½ cups) of the shredded cheese mixture. Simmer, stirring until slightly thickened, velvety, and smooth, about 4 minutes.

Add the cooked macaroni to the cheese mixture. Mix well, taste, and adjust the seasoning as needed. Cover and set aside.

Heat the avocado oil in a 12-inch cast-iron skillet over medium-high heat. Cook in batches to avoid overcrowding the pan. Add the chicken pieces and cook, turning once, until they are cooked through and have a golden-brown crust, about 5 minutes. Transfer to a plate, including any browned bits, and repeat with the remaining chicken, adding more oil as needed.

Preheat the oven to 400°F (200°C).

Continued on next page...

Recipe continued from previous page...

FOR THE MAC AND CHEESE

8 cups chicken broth

4 cups water

1 tablespoon kosher salt

16 ounces elbow macaroni

8 oz smoked Gouda, shredded

8 oz extra-sharp Cheddar cheese, shredded

½ cup unsalted butter

1 garlic clove, grated

1 cup half-and-half

1 can (12 oz) evaporated milk

1 tablespoon CajunSpice (substitution, page 13)

1 tablespoon WhiteSpice

1 tablespoon YardSpice

1 teaspoon freshly ground black pepper

1 teaspoon jerk seasoning, such as Walkerswood

—

1 tablespoon avocado oil, plus more if needed

1 green onion, green part only, finely chopped

Wipe out the skillet with paper towels. Add half the mac and cheese mixture to the skillet. Top with half the chicken and half the remaining shredded cheese mixture. Repeat, layering the remaining mac and cheese mixture, chicken, and shredded cheese. Cover the skillet with aluminum foil and bake until warmed through, about 30 minutes. Remove the foil and preheat the broiler. Place the skillet under the broiler and broil until the cheese is bubbling and browned, about 4 minutes.

Garnish with the green onion and serve at once.

JAMAICAN RICE & "PEAS"

MAKES 4–6 SERVINGS

1 can (15.5 oz) dark-red kidney beans, drained

2 cups water, divided

5 whole allspice berries

1-inch piece fresh ginger, peeled

1 Scotch bonnet chile

4 fresh thyme sprigs

1 clove garlic, smashed

1 green onion, halved, with ends trimmed

1 can (13.5 oz) coconut milk

2 tablespoons butter

1 teaspoon salt

2½ cups jasmine or basmati rice, rinsed and drained

Now, these are not the typical green peas you would find alongside, say, a helping of carrots. In Jamaica, we refer to all beans as peas. Don't ask me why; I don't make the rules, I just follow them. Here, I use canned beans because they are a helpful alternative to dried beans. Typically, red kidney beans are soaked overnight and then cooked for an hour before proceeding with the rice and other ingredients.

Place the beans in a medium-size pot. Add 1 cup of water to the can and swish it around to pick up any residue from the bottom, then pour it into the pot. Repeat with the remaining 1 cup of water.

Bring the beans to a boil over medium-high heat.

Add the allspice, ginger, Scotch bonnet (make sure it is whole and not pierced), thyme, garlic, and green onion. Reduce the heat to medium-low, cover, and cook for 6–8 minutes, until the color of the water deepens. Add the coconut milk, butter, and salt. Mix well and raise the heat to medium-high. Cook for 2–3 minutes longer, until combined.

Add the rice, stirring everything together until evenly combined. Reduce the heat to medium and cook, uncovered, for 8–12 minutes, until all the water has been absorbed.

Reduce the heat to low, cover, and cook for 10–15 minutes longer, until all of the water has evaporated. Remove from the heat, fluff the rice with a fork, and serve hot.

SWEET SAUSAGE SMASH BURGER

**MAKES 2 SERVINGS;
2 BURGERS**

1 lb sweet Italian sausage,
casings removed

2 brioche buns

2 slices pepper jack cheese

Sun-Dried Tomato Aioli
(page 149) for serving

4 leaves Bibb lettuce

1 Roma tomato, thinly sliced

I love sweet Italian sausage—one is guaranteed to always find it in my fridge or freezer. Smash burgers are common among New York delis, and I had the idea to try them with this sweet sausage. I hope you are as delighted by the result as I am.

Line a work surface with parchment paper or wax paper.

Using wet hands to prevent sticking, roll the sausage meat into balls, about the size of a golf ball, and use your palm to press them into 4-inch patties on the prepared work surface.

In a dry, medium cast-iron skillet over medium-high heat, toast the buns, then remove them from the skillet and set them aside.

In the same skillet, still over medium-high heat, lay out your sausage patties. Cook without moving them for 2 minutes, or until they release with ease. Flip and cook the patties for 2–3 minutes longer, until they begin brown and become firm. Add the cheese for the last minute of cooking, then remove the skillet from the heat. Cover and allow the cheese to melt.

Spread some aioli on the toasted bottom buns, then add 2 slices of Bibb lettuce, tomato slices, and a cooked sausage patty to each. Add the top bun and enjoy!

JAMAICAN OXTAIL

MAKES 4 SERVINGS

2 lb oxtail, washed well
(see tip page 82)

2 tablespoons dark soy sauce

1 tablespoon Jamaican Green
Seasoning (page 13)

1 tablespoon WhiteSpice
(substitution, page 13)

1 tablespoon YardSpice
(substitution, page 13)

1 tablespoon adobo seasoning

½ tablespoon salt, plus more
to taste

½ tablespoon freshly ground
black pepper

6 cloves garlic, minced

5 fresh thyme sprigs, divided

5 whole allspice berries

2 green onions, sliced into
thin rounds

1 small yellow onion, diced

1 Scotch bonnet chile, diced
(optional)

2–3 boxes (32 oz) beef broth
(optional)

1 bay leaf

Another one of Jamaica's well-known delicacies is our oxtail. It's commonly referred to as braised oxtail or oxtail stew—I just call it oxtail, and it's one of my favorite dishes. Decent cuts of oxtail should be available to purchase at your local butcher.

Place the oxtail in a large bowl. Season with the soy sauce, green seasoning, WhiteSpice, YardSpice, adobo seasoning, ½ tablespoon of salt, and the pepper.

Add the garlic, 2 sprigs of thyme, the allspice, green onions, yellow onion, and Scotch bonnet (if using). Using gloved hands (Scotch bonnets are extremely hot), mix well until every piece of the oxtail is well coated. Cover tightly and marinate in the refrigerator for at least 2 hours, although overnight to 48 hours is always preferred.

Bring a kettle of water to a boil—it is important that you have hot water at all times throughout the cooking process. Alternatively, place the beef broth in a medium saucepan and bring to a boil over high heat, then reduce the heat to maintain a simmer. (I like to use beef broth instead of water for additional flavor.)

In a Dutch oven or large pot (the Dutch oven will allow you to finish the oxtail in the oven, if desired) over medium-high heat, warm the coconut oil until melted. Add the ginger and cook, stirring constantly, for 2 minutes. This infuses the oil with ginger flavor. Add the marinated oxtail pieces, making sure they are spaced evenly so they can brown. Cook for 8–10 minutes on each side without moving them, until both sides are browned. Add the hot water or beef broth until the oxtail is covered and add the bay leaf. Reduce the heat to medium-low and cover. Cook until the liquid level reduces by about three-fourths, about 30 minutes. Add more water or beef broth and repeat this process until the oxtail is fork tender, about 1½–2 hours total cooking time.

Continued on next page...

Recipe continued from previous page...

3 tablespoons coconut oil

1-inch piece fresh ginger, peeled and minced

1 can (15.5 oz) butter beans, drained and rinsed

½ cup Grace ketchup

1 tablespoon beef bouillon

1 large carrot, peeled and cut into rounds

1 red bell pepper, diced

1 green bell pepper, diced

Jamaican Rice & "Peas" (page 77) for serving

Add the drained butter beans, remaining 3 sprigs of thyme, the carrot, red and green bell peppers, ketchup, additional salt to taste, and beef bouillon, mixing well.

Raise the heat to medium-high and cook for 15–20 minutes, until the sauce is thickened and the carrots are fork tender.

Serve hot with rice and peas and enjoy.

TASTEMAKER TIP: *Washing oxtail very well is a must. Washing the meat with a bit of vinegar, lukewarm water, and lime will help lift up any bone shards that may have gotten into the meat and cut through any sliminess on the oxtail.*

BROWN STEW CHICKEN

MAKES 4–6 SERVINGS

3 lb bone-in chicken legs and thighs, cut into pieces about 2-inches in size (see tip below)

6 cloves garlic, minced

5 fresh thyme sprigs

2-inch piece fresh ginger, peeled and minced

3 tablespoons Jamaican Green Seasoning (page 156)

2 tablespoons YardSpice (substitution, page 13)

2 tablespoons WhiteSpice (substitution, page 13)

2 tablespoons dark soy sauce

½ tablespoon salt

½ tablespoon ground black pepper

2 green onions, sliced into rounds

3 tablespoons coconut oil

2 tablespoons sugar

5 whole allspice berries

1 Scotch bonnet chile

1 large carrot, cut into ½-inch slices on the bias

1 tablespoon chicken bouillon

½ cup ketchup

Jamaican Rice & "Peas" (page 77) for serving

If someone asked me to name a meal that I could eat every day, it would be a hard fight between this stew chicken and curry chicken. What I love most about this recipe is how simple it seems but how many ingredients go into creating its unique flavor profile.

Place the chicken in a large bowl with a lid. Add the garlic, thyme, ginger, green seasoning, YardSpice, WhiteSpice, soy sauce, salt, and black pepper. Add the green onions, yellow onion, and green and red bell peppers.

Mix together well and allow the mixture to marinate in the refrigerator for at least 1 hour and up to overnight.

Bring a full kettle of water to a boil, then turn it down to maintain a simmer.

In a large heavy bottom pot, such as Dutch oven, over medium-high heat, melt the coconut oil. Add the sugar and cook, stirring constantly to prevent burning, until it is a deep caramel color, about 3–4 minutes.

Add the chicken, reserving the thyme, onion, and bell peppers in the bowl. Cook the chicken for 2 minutes, then add the allspice and Scotch bonnet. Reduce the heat to medium, cover the pot, and cook for 10–12 minutes, until the chicken has produced its own juices. Mix well, cover, and cook 5–6 minutes longer, until the juices begin to reduce.

Meanwhile, add the carrot to the bowl with the onions, bell peppers, and thyme. Scrape down the sides and pour in the hot water to cover.

Pour in all the water and vegetables from the bowl, then add the bouillon and ketchup. Cover and cook, still over medium heat, for 10–12 minutes, until the carrots are fork tender.

Mix gently so as not to break up the chicken, which should now be very tender. Taste and adjust the seasoning as needed.

Serve hot with rice and peas and enjoy.

TASTEMAKER TIP: *Because I prefer to use bone-in chicken for this recipe, I ask the butcher to cut it for me when I buy it.*

CHICKEN MEATBALLS WITH GARLIC BUTTER SAUCE & ORZO SALAD

MAKES 8–10 SERVINGS

2 lb ground chicken

1 cup panko bread crumbs

½ cup Italian-style bread crumbs

¼ cup grated Parmesan

1 tablespoon WhiteSpice (substitution, page 13)

1 tablespoon kosher salt

1 teaspoon freshly ground black pepper

½ cup diced shallots

½ head Perfect Roasted Garlic (page 150)

1 tablespoon chopped fresh flat-leaf parsley

1 large egg

½ cup half-and-half

Orzo Salad (page 116)

This was the very first recipe I created for this book, and what a way to get my culinary creativity wheels turning. These Chicken Meatballs are a total crowd-pleaser. The Garlic Butter Sauce and Orzo Salad are the perfect companions and help load each bite with exciting flavor.

Preheat the oven to 400°F (200°C). Line a baking sheet with aluminum foil. Spray with a light layer of cooking spray or brush with a light coating of olive oil.

In a large bowl, gently flake the ground chicken with a fork. Add the panko and Italian-style bread crumbs, Parmesan, WhiteSpice, salt, and pepper. Then add the shallots, roasted garlic, parsley, and egg. Add the half-and-half around the edges of the bowl. Wet your hands and gently mix the ingredients until blended.

Wet your hands again and, using a ⅓-cup measure, divide and roll the chicken mixture into meatballs. Place them on the prepared baking sheet. (It's important that all the meatballs are the same size so they cook through at the same time.)

Let the meatballs rest for 15 minutes, then bake for 12 minutes. They won't be completely cooked through at this point.

Place the garlic butter sauce in a small saucepan over medium heat.

Add the meatballs and baste with the sauce, reduce the heat to low, cover, and cook for 3–4 minutes, until cooked through.

Serve with the Orzo Salad and enjoy!

ONE-PAN MAPLE CHICKEN & RICE

MAKES 4 SERVINGS

1 lb skinless chicken thighs

¼ cup dark maple syrup

2 tablespoons sriracha

1 tablespoon dark soy sauce

1-inch piece fresh ginger, peeled and grated

1 teaspoon YardSpice (substitution, page 13)

1 teaspoon WhiteSpice (substitution, page 13)

2 tablespoons avocado oil

3 cloves garlic, minced

1 small red bell pepper, diced

1 small green bell pepper, diced

1 small yellow onion, diced

2 ribs celery, diced

3 fresh thyme sprigs

2 tablespoons butter

1½ cups long-grain rice

2½ cups Chicken Stock (page 159)

3 teaspoons salt

One-pan meals for the win, always. They limit both cleanup and cook time, while yielding a delicious and filling result. A rice dish like this one is also a great way to load up on your vegetables. Add mushrooms, spinach, kale, or whatever you like!

Preheat the oven to 350°F (180°C).

Add the chicken thighs to large bowl with a lid. Add the maple syrup, sriracha, soy sauce, ginger, YardSpice, and WhiteSpice. Mix until all the chicken is well coated. Marinate in the refrigerator for at least 30 minutes, and up to overnight.

In a large Dutch oven (or cast-iron skillet with an oven-safe lid) over medium-high heat, warm the avocado oil. Add the marinated chicken and cook for 4–6 minutes on each side, until browned.

Transfer the chicken to a plate.

Reduce the heat to medium and add the garlic, red and green bell peppers, onion, celery, and thyme and cook, stirring occasionally, for 2–3 minutes, until softened. Add the butter and rice and cook, stirring occasionally, for 3–5 minutes, until the color of the rice deepens and is a bit toasty. Season with salt.

Remove the Dutch oven from the heat and add the broth. Mix well, scraping up any brown bits on the bottom.

Add the chicken, nestling it into the rice mixture. Cover with the oven-safe lid and bake for 35–40 minutes, until the rice is fluffy and the chicken is cooked through.

Remove from the oven, fluff with a fork, and serve hot.

JUMP-START CHICKEN

MAKES 4 SERVINGS

¼ lb sliced bacon, chopped

4 cloves garlic, minced

1 small shallot, finely diced

1 large carrot, sliced into rounds

1 cup Chicken Stock (page 159)

1 can (10.5 oz) cream of chicken soup

1 tablespoon ZestySpice (substitution, page 13)

2 teaspoons CajunSpice (substitution, page 13)

2 teaspoons WhiteSpice (substitution, page 13)

3 fresh thyme sprigs

1 cup water, or as needed

1 store-bought rotisserie chicken, quartered

3 fresh flat-leaf parsley sprigs, chopped

Cooked rice for serving

This recipe is basically just a super tasty sauce that accompanies a store-bought rotisserie chicken—a convenient jump-start on your meal, hence the name. Some days we need to get dinner on the table as quickly as possible. Dressing up a rotisserie chicken takes the hassle out of slow cooking one at home and allows you to get something fab on the table quickly.

Place a large lidded skillet over medium-high heat. Add the bacon pieces and cook until crispy, 9–12 minutes. Transfer the bacon to a small bowl and set it aside, keeping the fat in the pan.

In the same skillet, add the garlic, shallot, and carrot and cook in the bacon fat for 4–5 minutes, until everything is softened and fragrant.

Deglaze the skillet with the chicken stock, then add the soup, ZestySpice, CajunSpice, and WhiteSpice.

Reduce the heat to medium, add the thyme, and mix until smooth. Add the water if the consistency is too thick. Cover and cook the sauce for 2–3 minutes, until you have a gravy-like texture.

Submerge the rotisserie chicken into the sauce and top with the parsley. Cover and cook for 2–3 minutes to reheat the chicken.

Top the cooked chicken with the bacon pieces. Serve with rice and enjoy.

RASTA RISOTTO

MAKES 4–6 SERVINGS

1 lb small shrimp, peeled and deveined

2 teaspoons salt, divided

2 teaspoons WhiteSpice, divided (substitution, page 13)

2 teaspoons YardSpice, divided (substitution, page 13)

1 teaspoon ground allspice

3 tablespoons jerk seasoning, divided

6 cups Chicken Stock (page 159)

2 tablespoons coconut oil, divided

1 large red bell pepper, diced

1 large green bell pepper, diced

1 large yellow bell pepper, diced

Scotch bonnet chile, diced (optional)

6 cloves garlic, minced

3 green onions, sliced into rounds

1-inch piece fresh ginger, peeled and minced

1 small yellow onion, diced

1 package (16 oz) orzo pasta

2 cups heavy cream

4 fresh thyme sprigs

¼ cup shredded Parmesan cheese

This elevated risotto is definitely one of my top five recipes in this book! A true "Oh, wow!" moment with an incredible mix of flavors and seasonings. This is the only time I'll suggest using small shrimp, as they make this dish easier to eat.

Place the shrimp in a medium bowl and season with 1 teaspoon of salt, 1 teaspoon of WhiteSpice, 1 teaspoon of YardSpice, ground allspice, and 1 tablespoon of jerk seasoning. Mix well and set aside to marinate for 30 minutes.

Place the stock in a medium saucepan over low heat to simmer.

Warm 1 tablespoon of coconut oil in a large skillet over medium-high heat. Add the marinated shrimp and cook for 3–4 minutes. Transfer to a bowl and set aside.

Add the remaining 1 tablespoon of coconut oil and melt it. Add the red, green, and yellow bell peppers, Scotch bonnet (if using), garlic, green onions, ginger, and yellow onion. Cook, stirring occasionally, for 4–6 minutes, until softened.

Add the orzo and stir vigorously for 1–2 minutes, ensuring the orzo is not sticking or burning. Ladle in some of the hot chicken stock, enough to cover the orzo, and reduce the heat to low. Cook, stirring occasionally to prevent sticking and adding stock as needed, until the orzo is al dente, about 25–30 minutes.

Add the heavy cream, the remaining 1 teaspoon of salt, 1 teaspoon of WhiteSpice, 1 teaspoon of YardSpice, 2 tablespoons of jerk seasoning, and the thyme. Mix well. Cook, stirring occasionally, for 2–3 minutes, until evenly combined. Add the shrimp and Parmesan and mix well.

Remove from the heat and enjoy!

BROWN BUTTER TORTELLINI

MAKES 2 SERVINGS

5 quarts water

1 tablespoon salt

1 package (20 oz) fresh cheese tortellini

½ cup butter

3 cloves garlic, smashed

1 fresh rosemary sprig

4 fresh sage leaves, chopped

Juice of ½ lemon

Grated Parmesan for serving

I'll find any excuse to brown some butter. The aroma that lingers afterward is wonderfully fragrant. Tortellini is an elite pasta in my eyes, especially during the winter months. I know winter pasta isn't a common concept, but this dish is truly like a warm hug on a cold day.

Bring the water and salt to a boil over high heat. Add the tortellini, reduce the heat to medium, and cook for 7–8 minutes, until they are al dente and float to the surface of the water.

Drain and set aside.

Place the butter in a large skillet over medium heat and melt it fully. Add the garlic and rosemary. Cook, stirring frequently to prevent the garlic and butter from burning, until the butter begins to foam, 2–3 minutes. Remove the garlic and rosemary and discard.

Continue stirring until the butter is brown, about 5 minutes longer, then immediately remove the pan from the heat.

Add the sage leaves and lemon juice and mix well.

Add the cooked tortellini and fold them in.

Top with some Parmesan cheese and enjoy!

GOCHUJANG CRAB NOODLES

MAKES 4 SERVINGS

8 oz instant noodles

3 cups lightly packed baby spinach

3 tablespoons gochujang

3 green onions, sliced into rounds

2 teaspoons sesame seeds

6 cloves garlic, grated

1-inch piece fresh ginger, peeled and grated

3 teaspoons brown sugar

1 tablespoon soy sauce

½ teaspoon salt

4 tablespoons avocado or vegetable oil

1 tablespoon butter

1 package (8 oz) lump crabmeat

You can't go wrong with a bowl of hot delicious noodles. These noodles are the perfect option for a weeknight dinner. I add lots of spinach for a healthy serving of greens. Bok choy is also a fabulous addition here, as it adds a satisfying crunch.

Boil the noodles according to the package instructions. Add the spinach for the last minute of cooking. Drain and place in a large bowl. Set aside.

In a small bowl, combine the gochujang, green onions, sesame seeds, garlic, ginger, brown sugar, soy sauce, and salt. Whisk together until evenly combined. Set aside.

In a small saucepan over medium heat, warm the avocado oil for 1–2 minutes, until hot. Pour the heated oil over the sauce mixture, whisking as you pour.

Set aside.

In a small skillet over medium heat, melt the butter. Add the crabmeat and cook, mixing gently, for 1 minute, until warmed through.

Add the cooked crab meat to the large bowl containing the spinach and noodles. Add the sauce mixture to the same bowl and toss together until thoroughly combined.

Serve hot and enjoy!

BBL FRIED CABBAGE

MAKES 4–6 SERVINGS

1 lb thick-cut bacon, cut into 1-inch pieces

13 oz smoked sausage, cut into half-moons

1 large yellow onion, thinly sliced lengthwise

1 large red bell pepper, thinly sliced lengthwise

1 large green bell pepper, thinly sliced lengthwise

1 teaspoon salt

6 cloves garlic, minced

1 tablespoon YardSpice (substitution, page 13)

2 teaspoons WhiteSpice (substitution, page 13)

Cooked rice for serving

This BBL Fried Cabbage is a great side dish, or you can enjoy it as an entrée served over rice. This recipe proved to be a favorite among my social media pages and I think it gained a lot of comments and views simply because of its name—what's understood doesn't need to be explained.

In a large dry skillet over medium-high heat, cook the bacon, stirring occasionally, for 8–9 minutes, until crispy. Transfer the bacon to a medium bowl and set aside, keeping all the fat in the pan.

In the same skillet, add sausage and cook for 2–3 minutes per side, until crispy. Add the sausage to the bowl with the bacon, keeping all the fat in the pan.

Add the onion and red and green peppers to the skillet and cook, stirring occasionally, for 3–4 minutes, until the vegetables are slightly softened but not mushy. Add the salt. Transfer the vegetables to the bowl with the sausage and bacon.

You should now have a generous amount of renderings in the skillet. Add the cabbage, a couple handfuls at a time, and cook for 1 minute before adding more. This allows the cabbage to fry and soften without steaming, which produces too much liquid. Once all the cabbage is in and softened, add the garlic, YardSpice, and WhiteSpice, and mix well. Cook for 1–2 minutes, until softened.

Reduce the heat to medium-low. Add the cooked bacon, sausage, onions, and peppers. Mix well.

Serve hot over rice and enjoy!

THREE SAUCE NAAN PIZZA WITH CRISPY PROSCIUTTO

**MAKES 2–4 SERVINGS;
2 NAAN PIZZAS**

4 thin slices prosciutto
(about 2 oz)

2 naan (about ½ lb total)

Olive oil for brushing and
drizzling

2 heaping tablespoons
basil pesto

2 heaping tablespoons
vodka sauce

2 heaping tablespoons
marinara sauce

1 cup shredded mozzarella
cheese

1 cup baby arugula

Kosher salt and freshly
ground black pepper

Between the light and fluffy naan, the crispy prosciutto, and the tangy marinara, it's hard to decide what makes these naan pizzas so delicious. Each ingredient here is really working together to achieve the cheesy, flavorful greatness. My favorite part, aside from eating it, is topping it off with that final sprinkle of salt and pepper and a smooth drizzle of olive oil.

Preheat the oven to 375°F (190°C). Line a baking sheet with parchment paper or a silicone mat.

Lay the prosciutto slices flat on the prepared baking sheet. Bake until crisp, 7–8 minutes. Remove from the baking sheet and set aside on a plate.

Brush the naan very lightly with olive oil on both sides. Arrange the naan on the baking sheet. Spread half of the pesto over the top of each naan. Spread half of the vodka sauce on half of each naan, then spread the marinara on the other half. Sprinkle on the mozzarella, dividing evenly between the naan.

Bake until the cheese has melted and the naan is golden, 8–10 minutes.

Transfer the naan pizzas to individual plates. Top each with half the arugula, then drizzle with olive oil and season with salt and pepper. Crumble the crispy prosciutto over the top, dividing evenly, and serve at once.

TURMERIC-GINGER BRANZINO

MAKES 2 SERVINGS

1 whole branzino (1 lb),
filleted and washed

3 teaspoons avocado oil,
divided

2 teaspoons WhiteSpice,
divided (substitution, page 13)

2 teaspoons YardSpice,
divided (substitution, page 13)

1 teaspoon ground mustard

½ teaspoon salt

1 teaspoon all-purpose flour

1 tablespoon coconut oil

2 teaspoons ground turmeric

½ teaspoon freshly ground
black pepper

3 whole allspice berries

2 cloves garlic, grated

2-inch piece fresh ginger,
peeled and halved

½ cup coconut cream

4 fresh thyme sprigs

I couldn't close this chapter without including a solid fish recipe. I lean on fish a lot, especially on weeknights when I need to get something on the table and may not have the bandwidth to cook for an hour. This recipe calls for a filleted branzino. I always ask for my fish to be filleted at the fish counter when I purchase it.

Place the branzino, skin-side down, on a clean surface lined with a paper towel and gently pat it dry.

Coat the fish in 1 teaspoon of avocado oil and season with 1 teaspoon of WhiteSpice, 1 teaspoon of YardSpice, the ground mustard, and salt. Rub the seasonings on the fish, then sprinkle on the flour, ensuring to pack everything on. This will help give the fish a great crust.

Warm the remaining 2 teaspoons of avocado oil in a medium skillet over medium-high heat. Add the branzino, skin-side up, and cook for 3 minutes on each side, until browned. Transfer the branzino to a clean surface.

Add the coconut oil to the pan, still over medium-high heat, and melt it. Add the turmeric, then immediately add the pepper to activate the turmeric. Stir rapidly for 1 minute, until the color of the turmeric deepens. Add the allspice, garlic, and ginger and cook, stirring occasionally, for 1 minute.

Add the coconut cream.

Reduce the heat to medium and add the thyme. Add the remaining 1 teaspoon of WhiteSpice and 1 teaspoon of YardSpice. Simmer the sauce for 3–4 minutes, until thickened.

Place the sauce on the bottom of a serving dish, then lay the fish, skin-side down, on the sauce. This will keep the fish warm and intact. Serve right away.

GARLICKY LEMON PEPPER LAMB CHOPS WITH HONEY GLAZE

MAKES 2 SERVINGS

2 lb lamb chops

2 tablespoons avocado oil, divided

3 cloves garlic, grated

2 tablespoons ZestySpice (substitution, page 13)

1 tablespoon WhiteSpice (substitution, page 13)

1 tablespoon CajunSpice (substitution, page 13)

1 teaspoon salt

1 teaspoon freshly ground black pepper

FOR THE GLAZE

3 tablespoons water

2 tablespoons butter

¼ cup honey

2 teaspoons Dijon mustard

2 teaspoons WhiteSpice

1 fresh thyme sprig

—

Chopped fresh flat-leaf parsley for garnish

If you secretly want your dinner guests to rave about your cooking skills long after the table is cleared, give these juicy and tender lamb chops a try. Fair warning, they are addictive. So, as the newly designated maker of delicious lamb chops, prepare to be heckled to make them often from then on.

Place the lamb chops in a large bowl with a lid. Add 1 tablespoon of avocado oil. Add the garlic, ZestySpice, WhiteSpice, CajunSpice, salt, and pepper. Mix well to coat the lamb chops and marinate in the refrigerator for 1–2 hours.

In a skillet large enough for the chops to have a ½ inch of space between them, warm the remaining 1 tablespoon of avocado oil over medium-high heat. Add the lamb chops and cook for 4–5 minutes on each side, until an instant-read thermometer inserted into the thickest part of the chop registers 145°F (63°C). Transfer the lamb chops to a serving platter. Cover with aluminum foil and allow to rest for 10 minutes while you make the glaze.

To make the glaze, in the same pan, reduce the heat to medium and add the water and butter to deglaze it, scraping up any brown bits on the bottom. Add the honey, mustard, WhiteSpice, and thyme. Cook, whisking constantly, until the sauce bubbles and begins to form a glaze-like consistency, about 2–3 minutes.

Glaze the lamb chops immediately, garnish with parsley, and serve hot.

SOUL BOWL SERIES

Soul food is such an important part of Black culture. The name became popular among the Black community in the 1960s, when the word "soul" was a popular word used to describe our character, style, and music. The recipes and methods for cooking soul food are often passed down from generation to generation. Soul food can consist of many different main and side dishes, such as the smothered chicken, sweet potatoes, collard greens, black-eyed peas, and rice that you will find in this series. And those are just a few. Soul food brings us together. It soothes and nourishes our bodies. It is well-seasoned, made with love, served hot, and feeds the soul.

To date, the Soul Bowl is one of my highest performing videos across all social media. It's the dish that is most frequently re-created by my amazing supporters and followers. It is all you need in one delicious, hearty bowl.

Before we begin, to make your cooking experience as seamless as possible, I'll share an order of preparation that I've found works best. I suggest making the turkey-neck broth first—it will take the longest to cook and the extra time will ensure that the cooked meat is at its most tender. Follow that with marinating the chicken, then make the sweet potatoes. Move on to the kale, then the black-eyed peas, and, finally, cooking the chicken.

Everyone has their way of preparing soul food, and I am delighted to share my way with you.

- COLLARD KALE WITH SMOKED TURKEY-NECK BROTH
- HOLY TRINITY RICE
- ROASTED SWEET POTATOES
- BLACK-EYED PEAS
- CREAMY CAJUN CHICKEN

COLLARD KALE WITH SMOKED TURKEY-NECK BROTH

MAKES 6 SERVINGS

2 lb smoked turkey necks
or 1 smoked turkey leg

1 tablespoon chicken bouillon

1 tablespoon apple cider
vinegar

1 teaspoon whole
peppercorns

2 cloves garlic, smashed

1 bay leaf

½ tablespoon WhiteSpice
(substitution, page 13)

½ tablespoon CajunSpice
(substitution, page 13)

4 tablespoons hot sauce,
divided

1 lb (5 large stalks) kale

4 tablespoons white vinegar,
divided

Salt

Now, as much as I adore soul food, I am simply not a fan of collard greens or ham hocks. I am, however, all about this Collard Kale variation. Traditional collard greens are typically slow cooked overnight in a large pot with ham hocks added for flavor. This Collard Kale takes less time to cook, while allowing you to indulge in the same flavors and add more nutrients.

Add the turkey necks to a large pot and cover them with about 2 inches of water. Add the chicken bouillon, apple cider vinegar, whole peppercorns, and garlic. Bring the mixture to a boil over medium-high heat, then add the bay leaf, WhiteSpice, CajunSpice, and 2 tablespoons of hot sauce. Reduce the heat to medium and cover. Cook for 45 minutes, allowing the water to cloud.

Meanwhile, cut the kale leaves away from the thick woody stems and discard the stems.

Plug the sink and fill it with warm water. Add 2 tablespoons of white vinegar. Add the kale leaves, swishing them around and massaging the kale to remove any impurities. Rinse the kale with fresh water in a colander. Allow the kale to drain a bit, then transfer it to a clean cutting board. Roll a few leaves together tightly and slice into ½-inch-thick ribbons.

When the turkey necks are done, remove them from the broth and, using 2 forks, shred the meat from the bones. Discard the bones and return the meat to the pot, along with the kale. Add the remaining 2 tablespoons of hot sauce and 2 tablespoons of white vinegar. Season to taste with salt.

Reserve 2 cups of broth and a ¼ cup of shredded meat for the Black-Eyed Peas (page 105).

HOLY TRINITY RICE

MAKES 6 SERVINGS

2 tablespoons butter

1 tablespoon olive oil

6 cloves garlic, minced

3 ribs celery, finely diced

1 small green bell pepper, finely diced

1 small white onion, finely diced

2½ cups long-grain rice, rinsed well and drained

2 teaspoons CajunSpice (substitution, page 13)

2 teaspoons WhiteSpice (substitution, page 13)

2 teaspoons salt

4 cups Chicken Stock (page 159)

2 bay leaves

This rice is the foundation of the Soul Bowl. It's so fluffy and delicious, it can be enjoyed on its own. The Holy Trinity Rice will act as the bed for the rest of the Soul Bowl elements. It makes a perfect catch-all for the drops of flavor that will attempt to sneak to the bottom of your bowl.

Warm the butter and olive oil in a medium-size lidded pot over medium-high heat.

Add the garlic, celery, bell pepper, and onion and cook, stirring occasionally, for 2–3 minutes, until the celery and onions are translucent and the bell peppers are softened.

Add the rice and cook, stirring occasionally, for 3–5 minutes, until the rice begins to toast and becomes golden. Add the CajunSpice, WhiteSpice, and salt.

Pour in the stock and mix well. Add the bay leaves. Cover and cook, still over medium-high heat, for 3–5 minutes, until the liquid evaporates. Reduce the heat to low, cover tightly, and allow the rice to steam for 12–15 minutes, until fluffy.

Remove from the heat, fluff the rice with a fork, and enjoy!

ROASTED SWEET POTATOES

MAKES 6 SERVINGS

2 lb sweet potatoes, peeled and cubed

Olive oil for brushing

1 tablespoon WhiteSpice (substitution, page 13)

1 teaspoon freshly ground black pepper

The Roasted Sweet Potatoes are perhaps my favorite element of the Soul Bowl. They're the subtle sweetness that helps balance the savory flavor. Often, when preparing traditional soul food, sweet potatoes are chopped and baked in a dish with lots of brown sugar and butter. This roasted version is a healthier alternative.

Preheat the oven to 400°F (200°C). Line a baking sheet with parchment paper.

Bring a large pot of water to a boil over high heat. Add the potatoes and boil for 4–6 minutes, until fork tender. Drain well.

Transfer the potatoes to the prepared baking sheet. Brush with olive oil and season with the WhiteSpice and pepper.

Bake, flipping the potatoes halfway through, for 45 minutes, until a crispy outer layer is formed.

BLACK-EYED PEAS

MAKES 6 SERVINGS

2 tablespoons butter

2 teaspoons olive oil

4 cloves garlic, minced

1 small white onion, diced

1 small green bell pepper, diced

1 can (15 oz) black-eyed peas, drained and rinsed

¼ cup shredded turkey neck (reserved from previous recipe, page 102)

2 cups smoked turkey-neck broth (page 102)

1 bay leaf

I could easily eat these Black-Eyed Peas with rice daily! There is an old superstition that says if you start the New Year with a fresh pot of black-eyed peas, you welcome a year of joy, luck, and prosperity—that's exactly what I felt in deciding to add these flavorful peas to the Soul Bowl.

In a medium pot over medium-high heat, warm the butter and olive oil together. Add the garlic, onion, and bell pepper and cook, stirring occasionally, for 2–3 minutes, until softened and fragrant. Add the peas and cook for 1 minute longer.

Add the turkey neck, broth, and bay leaf. Mix well. Reduce the heat to medium-low, cover, and cook for 25 minutes, until the broth thickens and the liquid reduces.

CREAMY CAJUN CHICKEN

MAKES 6 SERVINGS

1½ lb boneless, skinless
chicken thighs, cubed

2 tablespoons CajunSpice,
divided (substitution, page 13)

1½ tablespoons WhiteSpice,
divided (substitution, page 13)

1½ tablespoons YardSpice,
divided (substitution, page 13)

1 teaspoon salt

½ teaspoon ground black
pepper

1 tablespoon olive oil

2 tablespoons butter

6 cloves garlic, minced

3 ribs celery, finely diced

1 small white onion, finely
diced

1 small green bell pepper,
finely diced

2 cups heavy cream

And now, to seal the deal, the final component of the Soul Bowl. This rich and seasoned Creamy Cajun Chicken ties it all together and adds the perfect depth to this dish. The delicious scent alone that will waft through your kitchen while making this meal will leave you wanting to make it again. She's the bow on top of the gift, the cherry on top of the sundae.

Place the cubed chicken in a medium bowl with a lid. Season with 1 tablespoon of CajunSpice, ½ tablespoon of WhiteSpice, ½ tablespoon of YardSpice, the salt, and black pepper. Mix well and allow the chicken to marinate at room temperature for 35–45 minutes.

In a large skillet over high heat, warm the olive oil. Add the chicken pieces and cook for 2–3 minutes on each side, until browned. Transfer to a bowl and set aside.

Reduce the heat to medium-high and add the butter, scraping up any brown bits, then add the garlic, celery, onion, and bell pepper and cook, stirring occasionally, for 2–3 minutes, until they are fragrant.

Pour in the heavy cream and season with the remaining 1 tablespoon of CajunSpice, 1 tablespoon of WhiteSpice, and 1 tablespoon of YardSpice.

Mix well and add the cooked chicken. Cook, uncovered, for 4–5 minutes, until the sauce is thick enough to coat the back of a spoon.

Good & Guilt Free

BOOSTED BREAKFAST BOWL   111

CAULIFLOWER SOUTHWEST SKILLET
WITH CHIPOTLE SAUCE   112

CALLALOO STEW   115

ORZO SALAD   116

LEMONGRASS GROUND TURKEY   117

SPINACH & ARTICHOKE ZUCCHINI BOATS   118

STEAK-WRAPPED ASPARAGUS   121

CUCUMBER CRAB ROUNDS   122

GRILLED HALLOUMI SALAD WITH TAHINI DRESSING   123

ZUCCHINI & GREEN ONION FRITTERS   125

JAMAICAN STEAMED CABBAGE   126

GARLIC-GINGER BOK CHOY   127

BOOSTED BREAKFAST BOWL

MAKES 2 SERVINGS

FOR THE DRESSING

2 teaspoons white miso paste

2 teaspoons water

2 teaspoons tahini

2 teaspoons rice vinegar

1 teaspoon honey or agave, or to taste

1 teaspoon sriracha, or to taste

—

2–4 large eggs

4 thick-cut strips bacon, cut crosswise into ½-inch-thick strips

2 garlic cloves, minced

1 can (15 oz) black beans, drained and rinsed

Kosher salt and freshly ground black pepper

2 green onions, white and green parts, thinly sliced

1 bunch (6–7 oz) lacinato kale, stemmed and chopped

1 avocado, halved, pitted, peeled, and sliced

Maldon sea salt for garnish

My favorite detail about this breakfast bowl is that it's super customizable. It's simple and can be dressed way up if you want to add a bit of flare. Get creative with what you add. Some days, I use sautéed spinach instead of kale. You can top the bowl with sunflower seeds for a delightful added crunch.

To make the dressing, in a medium bowl, whisk together the miso, water, tahini, rice vinegar, honey, and sriracha until smooth. Set aside.

Bring a small saucepan two-thirds full of water to a boil over high heat. Add the eggs and reduce the heat to medium. Cook for 8 minutes for a jammy egg or 12 minutes for a hard-boiled egg. Drain the water and add ice and water to the saucepan. Let stand for 1 minute, then peel the eggs. Set aside.

In a medium frying pan over medium heat, cook the bacon, stirring occasionally, until crispy, about 6 minutes. Using a slotted spoon, transfer the bacon to paper towels to drain. Pour off all but 1 tablespoon of the bacon fat.

Add the garlic to the bacon fat and cook, still over medium heat, stirring to scrape up the browned bits on the pan bottom, until fragrant, about 30 seconds. Add the beans and season with salt and pepper. Cook, stirring occasionally, until warmed through, 2–3 minutes. Add the green onions and cook, stirring, for 1 minute. Remove from the heat.

Place the kale in another medium bowl and gently massage until tender. Add the kale to the bowl with the dressing and toss to coat evenly. Divide the kale between 2 individual serving bowls.

Spoon the bean mixture over the kale, dividing evenly. Halve the eggs. Arrange the eggs and sliced avocado on top of the beans, dividing evenly between the bowls. Season with salt and pepper. Sprinkle half the bacon over each serving and serve at once.

CAULIFLOWER SOUTHWEST SKILLET WITH CHIPOTLE SAUCE

MAKES 6 SERVINGS

2 tablespoons unsalted butter, divided

2 tablespoons avocado oil, divided

1 lb frozen riced cauliflower

1 tablespoon WhiteSpice (substitution, page 13)

1 tablespoon chili powder

1 teaspoon ground cumin

Kosher salt

1 small red onion, finely chopped

1 small red bell pepper, finely chopped

1 small orange bell pepper, finely chopped

1 small yellow bell pepper, finely chopped

1 small jalapeño, seeded and finely chopped

3 cloves garlic, minced

1 tablespoon CajunSpice (substitution, page 13)

1 cup fresh or frozen sweet corn kernels

1 can (15 oz) black beans, drained and rinsed

3 tablespoons water

¼ cup minced fresh cilantro

1½ cups shredded sharp Cheddar cheese or Monterey Jack-Cheddar blend

Chipotle Sauce (page 155) for serving

Whenever I can use a bit of a reset, or just need to take a step back from excess meat and carbs—my absolute favorite things—I reach for this skillet. The toppings can vary. Sometimes I top it with diced tomatoes or guacamole. The last time, I made toasted tortilla strips to add some crunch.

Preheat the oven to 400°F (200°C).

In a 10- or 12-inch cast-iron skillet over medium-high heat, warm 1 tablespoon of butter and 1 tablespoon of avocado oil. Add the cauliflower and cook, stirring occasionally, until softened, about 3 minutes. Stir in the WhiteSpice, chili powder, and cumin. Season with salt. Cook, stirring, until fragrant, about 1 minute. Transfer to a large bowl and set aside.

Place the remaining 1 tablespoon of avocado oil in the skillet over medium-high heat. Add the onion, red, orange, and yellow bell peppers, jalapeño, and garlic. Cook, stirring occasionally, until softened and starting to brown, 8–10 minutes. Stir in the CajunSpice, season with salt, and cook for 1 minute longer. Transfer to the bowl with the cauliflower.

Add the remaining 1 tablespoon of butter to the skillet over medium-high heat. Add the corn, beans, and water, then season with salt. Cook, stirring, until warmed through, about 3 minutes. Transfer the mixture and any juices to the bowl with the cauliflower. Add the cilantro and stir to combine.

Transfer the cauliflower mixture to the skillet and press into an even layer. Top evenly with the cheese. Bake until warmed through and the cheese is melted and bubbling, about 20 minutes.

Serve hot, passing the chipotle sauce alongside.

CALLALOO STEW

MAKES 4-6 SERVINGS

3 tablespoons coconut oil

1 tablespoon curry powder

1-inch piece fresh ginger, peeled

2 cups diced carrots

1 yellow onion, diced

3-4 green onions, sliced into small rounds (1 cup)

4 cloves garlic, minced

2 teaspoons salt, divided

2 teaspoons ground turmeric

1 teaspoon ground black pepper

1 can (13.5 oz) coconut milk

1½ cups Chicken Stock (page 159)

5 fresh thyme sprigs

4 whole allspice berries

1 can (19 oz) callaloo, drained

3 cups lightly packed broccoli florets

½ large green bell pepper, 1-inch cubed

½ large red bell pepper, 1-inch cubed

Cooked rice for serving

This callaloo stew came from my love for panang curry that I used to get from a local Thai take-out place, and, of course, my desire to get creative in the kitchen. The flavors are so bold, and I immediately wanted to marry the flavors of the curry with a staple flavor of the islands, callaloo.

Warm the coconut oil in a large pot over medium-high heat until melted and fragrant. Add the curry powder and ginger. Stir vigorously until the curry's color deepens and it becomes fragrant.

Add the carrots, yellow onion, green onions, and garlic. Season with 1 teaspoon of salt and cook, stirring occasionally, for 3-4 minutes longer. Add the turmeric, then add the black pepper to activate the turmeric. Mix well.

Pour in the coconut milk and stock. Add the thyme, allspice, callaloo, broccoli, green and red bell peppers, and remaining teaspoon of salt. Mix everything together well.

Reduce the heat to medium-low, cover, and cook for 3-4 minutes, until the dish attains a stew-like consistency.

Serve hot with rice and enjoy!

ORZO SALAD

MAKES 4–6 SERVINGS

1 package (16 oz) orzo pasta

1 lb asparagus, cut into 1-inch pieces

1 cup mayonnaise

⅓ cup fresh-squeezed lemon juice

1 tablespoon finely grated lemon zest

1 teaspoon sugar

1 teaspoon freshly ground black pepper

1 teaspoon kosher salt

½ cup chopped fresh dill

1½ tablespoons chopped fresh flat-leaf parsley

1½ cups chopped arugula

⅓ cup finely diced shallots

This is an all-purpose, all-season, all-occasion pasta salad. Fancy luncheon with your friends? Orzo Salad. Dinner with your parents? Orzo Salad. A cute solo brunch at home? Orzo Salad. It pairs perfectly with so many dishes. I love eating it with the Chicken Meatballs with Garlic Butter Sauce (page 84).

In a medium saucepan over medium-high heat, cook the orzo according to the package instructions, then drain and rinse under cold water. Set aside.

Prepare a large bowl of ice and water (an ice bath) to blanch the asparagus pieces. Bring a medium pot of water to a boil over medium-high heat. Add the asparagus and cook for 2 minutes, until bright green and tender. Drain the asparagus and transfer to the ice bath for 2–3 minutes. This stops the cooking process and allows the asparagus to stay green and crisp. Drain the asparagus again and set aside.

In a separate large bowl, whisk together the mayonnaise, lemon juice, lemon zest, sugar, pepper, and salt until smooth. Add the dill and parsley and mix until incorporated. Add the cooked orzo, asparagus, arugula, and shallot. Mix until evenly combined. Taste and add more salt as needed.

LEMONGRASS GROUND TURKEY .

MAKES 3–4 SERVINGS

2 tablespoons coconut oil, divided

1 lb 93%-lean ground turkey

½ tablespoon curry powder

½ tablespoon ground turmeric

1 teaspoon ground cumin

1 teaspoon ground black pepper

1 stalk lemongrass, bruised (see tip)

6 cloves garlic, minced

1-inch piece fresh ginger, peeled and minced

1 small shallot, finely diced

1 can (13.5 oz) coconut milk

¼ cup water

1 small red bell pepper, chopped into ½-inch pieces

1 small green bell pepper, chopped into ½-inch pieces

1 can (15.5 oz) chickpeas, drained and rinsed

1 tablespoon salt

2 teaspoons WhiteSpice (substitution, page 13)

2 tablespoons chilli garlic sauce, such as Lee Kum Kee brand

1 green onion, green part only, cut into rounds

Bibb lettuce leaves or cooked rice for serving

I love using this mixture for lettuce wraps. Grab some Bibb lettuce and your favorite toppings and you basically have a low-carb burrito. You can make it as spicy, mild, or sweet as you like. For a healthy option that stays packed with flavor, this recipe is easy to incorporate into your meal rotation.

In a large lidded skillet over medium heat, melt 1 tablespoon of coconut oil. Add the ground turkey and cook for about 3–4 minutes, until browned. Transfer the turkey to a medium bowl and set aside.

Add the remaining 1 tablespoon of coconut oil to the skillet, reduce the heat to medium-low, and melt the oil. Add the curry powder and turmeric and cook, mixing together, until their color deepens from a bright yellow to a deep nutty brown, 2–3 minutes. Add the black pepper to activate the turmeric, then add the cumin and cook and stir for 1 minute.

Add the lemongrass, garlic, ginger, and shallot and cook, stirring occasionally, for 2–3 minutes, until softened and fragrant. Add the coconut milk, chili garlic sauce, mixing everything together well, then add the water, red and green bell peppers, and chickpeas. Season with the salt and WhiteSpice. Mix well.

Return the turkey to the skillet. Cover and simmer for 3–4 minutes, allowing flavors to combine. Remove from the heat and discard the wooden stems of the lemongrass. Top with the green onion.
Serve with Bibb lettuce for lettuce wraps or over rice.

TASTEMAKER TIP: *To bruise the lemongrass, on a cutting board, using the back of a metal or wooden spoon, repeatedly beat along the stalk of the lemongrass until it becomes visibly limp and softened.*

SPINACH & ARTICHOKE ZUCCHINI BOATS

MAKES 3 SERVINGS

3 large zucchini

1½ cups shredded mozzarella cheese, divided

3 cups lightly packed chopped spinach

1 cup artichokes in oil, plus a bit of the oil for cooking

2 cloves garlic, grated

1 shallot, finely diced

1 package (8 oz) cream cheese

1 teaspoon salt

½ teaspoon freshly ground pepper

2 teaspoon YardSpice (substitution, page 13)

Last fall, I traveled to a farm out in eastern Long Island, near Wading River, and left with an abundance of fruits and vegetables including fresh, delicious zucchini. These boats are a result of that harvest. Getting vegetables in is important and it helps when they are well-seasoned, mixed with cheese, and baked to perfection.

Preheat the oven to 400°F (200°C). Grease a standard 9 x 12-inch baking dish.

Halve the zucchini lengthwise, then use a small spoon to scoop out the inner flesh of the zucchini and reserve it. Be gentle when scooping and try to smooth out the middle as much as possible. Place the zucchini boats in the prepared dish, hallowed-side up.

Evenly divide ½ cup of the mozzarella among the zucchini boats and bake for 8–10 minutes, until the cheese is visibly melted. Remove from the oven.

Meanwhile, in a medium skillet over medium heat, add the spinach, artichokes and oil, garlic, shallot, and reserved zucchini flesh and cook until softened, about 2–3 minutes.

Add the cream cheese, allowing it to soften, then add the salt, pepper, and YardSpice. Remove from the heat and mix everything together.

When the zucchini boats are done and removed from the oven, turn on the broiler.

Fill the boats with the spinach mixture, and then top with the remaining mozzarella.

Broil, uncovered, on the center rack for about 8 minutes, watching closely and allowing the zucchini to lose most of its moisture, until the cheese is bubbly and golden.

STEAK-WRAPPED ASPARAGUS

**MAKES 4–6 SERVINGS
(12 BUNDLES)**

2 teaspoons avocado oil

1½ teaspoons WhiteSpice
(substitution, page 13)

1½ teaspoons CajunSpice
(substitution, page 13)

6–8 oz London broil steak,
fat trimmed

1 bunch (about 1 lb) medium
asparagus spears, tough ends
snapped off

Salt and freshly ground
black pepper

5 tablespoons unsalted butter

**These perfectly seasoned asparagus spears wrapped in tender
pieces of meat just seem like a no-brainer. They are a delicious,
low carb, high-protein snack or appetizer. The trick is to wrap each
piece of steak around the asparagus diagonally, so it does not
overlap and cooks evenly.**

In a small bowl, stir together the avocado oil, WhiteSpice, and CajunSpice
to form a paste.

Slice the steak very thinly, about ¼-inch thick. You will need 1 slice for every
asparagus bundle, so about 12 slices.

One at a time, lay a piece of steak between 2 sheets of parchment paper.
Using a meat mallet, gently pound the steak to a ⅛-inch thickness. It
should be around 6 inches long and 1½–2 inches wide.

Brush the top side of each piece of steak with the spice paste, about
¼ teaspoon for each. For each, lay 2 asparagus spears on a piece of steak,
then, starting near the bottom of the spears, roll the steak around the
spears diagonally. Season the outside of the steak with salt and pepper.
Use a toothpick or kitchen string to secure the steak.

Warm a large heavy skillet over medium-high heat. Add half the butter and
swirl to coat the bottom of the pan. Add half the steak-asparagus bundles
and cook, turning once or twice, until the steak is seared all over, about 3
minutes. Cover the pan to finish steaming the asparagus until crisp-tender,
about 1 minute more.

Transfer to a plate and serve at once. Repeat with the remaining half of the
butter to cook the remaining bundles.

CUCUMBER CRAB ROUNDS

MAKES 2–3 SERVINGS

2 hard-boiled eggs

1 tablespoon capers

2 ribs celery, finely diced

1 small shallot, finely diced

1 cup light mayonnaise

2 tablespoons Dijon mustard

1 tablespoon sweet relish

1 tablespoon chopped fresh chives

1 tablespoon chopped fresh dill

2–3 teaspoons hot sauce

1 teaspoon cayenne pepper

1 teaspoon smoked paprika

1 teaspoon salt

½ teaspoon ground black pepper

1 package (8 oz) lump crabmeat

1 large English cucumber, sliced into 1-inch rounds

Sriracha for topping (optional)

This snack is versatile, since it can be presented as fancy or as casual as you'd like. I've served it as a dip at dinner parties with cocktails and rosemary crackers. I've also notoriously eaten this in bed with *Real Housewives* in the background and a family-size box of Wheat Thins. It's all about balance, my friends.

Coarsely chop the eggs and capers together, then transfer them to a large bowl. Add the celery, shallot, mayonnaise, mustard, relish, chives, dill, and hot sauce. Add the cayenne pepper, paprika, salt, and black pepper. Mix well until evenly combined and smooth.

Add the crabmeat and gently fold it in so it doesn't break down too much.

Scoop out about 1 tablespoon of the crab mixture onto each cucumber round and top with sriracha, if using.

GRILLED HALLOUMI SALAD WITH TAHINI DRESSING

MAKES 2–3 SERVINGS

8 oz Halloumi cheese, sliced into ½-inch-thick pieces

½ cup pine nuts

⅓ cup fresh arugula

4 mini cucumbers, thinly sliced

1 cup mixed olives

1 cup grape tomatoes, halved

1 shallot, thinly sliced

FOR THE DRESSING

2 tablespoons tahini

3 tablespoons honey

2 teaspoons water

Juice of 1 large lemon

1 teaspoon dried oregano

2 fresh dill sprigs, chopped

2 teaspoons red wine vinegar

4 teaspoons olive oil

As a kid, I loved salads, but I haven't been as fond of them as an adult. Recently, I've fallen back in love with making entrée salads—especially if I can utilize leftover ingredients that are already cut and on hand. This Halloumi salad has been in heavy rotation. Sometimes, I add herby grilled chicken and cooked farro for some flare.

In a dry grill pan over medium-high heat, grill the Halloumi for 2–3 minutes per side, until grill marks appear. Set aside. Add the pine nuts and toast, shaking the pan occasionally, for 2–3 minutes, until golden brown. Transfer the toasted nuts to a small bowl to cool.

Place the arugula in a large bowl. Add the cucumbers, olives, tomatoes, and shallot. Sprinkle on the toasted pine nuts, then top with the grilled halloumi cheese.

To make the dressing, in small bowl combine the tahini, honey, and water and whisk together until smooth. Add the lemon juice, oregano, dill, and red wine vinegar. Whisk in the olive oil slowly until evenly blended.

Pour the dressing over the salad, toss thoroughly, and enjoy.

ZUCCHINI & GREEN ONION FRITTERS

MAKES 3 SERVINGS

1 cup plain Greek yogurt

1 teaspoon fresh lemon juice

1 teaspoon minced fresh dill

½ teaspoon kosher salt, plus more to taste

2 zucchini, trimmed (about ¾ lb total)

2 green onions, white and green parts, thinly sliced

1 clove garlic, minced

2 large eggs, lightly beaten

3 tablespoons cornstarch

2 tablespoons all-purpose flour

¼ cup avocado or canola oil

Freshly ground black pepper

The trick to making these fritters good and guilt-free is using more eggs and less flour to bind them together. They are light and crispy on the outside and soft on the inside. They're just incredible and taste delicious with a sprinkle of flaky salt and dill, or Sun Dried Tomato Aioli (page 149).

In a small bowl, stir together the yogurt, lemon juice, and dill. Season with salt and pepper. Refrigerate until ready to use.

Using the large holes on a box grater, shred the zucchini into a fine-mesh sieve. Sprinkle the zucchini with ½ teaspoon of salt and toss to coat evenly. Set aside for 20 minutes.

Pour the zucchini onto cheesecloth, gather up the edges of the cheesecloth, and wring out as much liquid as you can, until the zucchini is dry and flaky. Transfer the zucchini to a medium bowl. Add the green onions and garlic and toss to combine. Add the eggs, ½ teaspoon salt, and a few grinds of pepper and stir gently to combine. Sprinkle the cornstarch and flour over the mixture and stir to combine.

Heat the avocado oil in a large nonstick or well-seasoned skillet over medium heat. Using a ¼-cup measure, scoop up mounds of the zucchini mixture and add them to the skillet; you should have 6–8 mounds. Cook, turning a few times, until golden brown on both sides and cooked through, about 6 minutes total.

Transfer to paper towels to drain and immediately season with salt and pepper.

Serve warm with the yogurt sauce.

JAMAICAN STEAMED CABBAGE

MAKES 4–6 SERVINGS

2 tablespoons coconut oil

5 fresh thyme sprigs

3 cloves garlic, minced

2 green onions, sliced into rounds

1 yellow onion, thinly sliced

¼–½ Scotch bonnet chile, finely diced

1 large white cabbage, cored and cut into thin strips

2–3 carrots, shredded

2 tablespoons butter (optional)

1 tablespoon YardSpice (substitution, page 13)

1 teaspoon salt

½ teaspoon freshly ground black pepper

Cooked rice for serving

Cooked protein of choice for serving

This steamed cabbage is both a side and a main dish in Jamaica. Sometimes it's served alongside a delicious cut of salted cod fish. It's incredible and packed with flavor. The carrots hold a bit of crunch that is satisfying with each bite, and the DinnerPlus seasonings really take this up a notch.

In a large lidded skillet over medium-high heat, melt the coconut oil. Add the thyme, garlic, green onions, yellow onion, and Scotch bonnet and cook, stirring continuously to prevent burning, for 1–2 minutes to infuse the oil with flavor.

Reduce the heat to medium-low. Add the cabbage, shredded carrots, and butter (if using). Cover the pan and steam the cabbage until softened, 12–16 minutes.

Season with the YardSpice, salt, and pepper.

Serve hot with rice and a protein of your choice.

GARLIC-GINGER BOK CHOY

MAKES 3–4 SERVINGS

1 tablespoon avocado oil

2 lb baby bok choy, halved lenghtwise

3 cloves garlic, grated

1–2-inch piece fresh ginger, peeled and grated

1 tablespoon sesame oil

½ tablespoon dark soy sauce

1 teaspoon WhiteSpice (substitution, page 13)

A quick and clean staple for me! I can easily eat bowls of this, especially over a bed of seasoned white rice. Bok choy has a mild and fresh flavor that is elevated with the bold notes of garlic and ginger. Try it with your favorite soup, salad, or stir-fry.

In a wok over high heat, warm the avocado oil. Add the bok choy and cook without touching for 1 minute, until a little char develops. Add the garlic and ginger and cook, stirring occasionally, for 1–2 minutes longer.

Add the sesame oil, soy sauce, and WhiteSpice. Give the wok a shake and then stir to combine.

Remove from the heat and serve hot!

Something Sweet

STRAWBERRY CHEESECAKE COOKIES   131

S'MORES DIP   132

PEAR SPICE CAKE WITH BOURBON GLAZE   134

CREAMY NO-BAKE CHEESECAKE BITES   135

SALTED CARAMEL PRETEZL BLONDIES   136

BLUEBERRY-COMPOTE BUTTER-CRUNCH CAKE   139

CRISPY CORNFLAKE SQUARES   140

BISCUIT DOUGHNUTS WITH LEMON GLAZE   141

STRAWBERRY CHEESECAKE COOKIES

MAKES 12–14 SERVINGS

1 cup all-purpose flour

1 cup graham cracker crumbs, plus 1–2 tablespoons for garnish

½ teaspoon baking soda

½ cup unsalted butter, at room temperature

½ cup granulated sugar

½ cup firmly packed light brown sugar

¼ teaspoon kosher salt

1 large egg

1½ teaspoons pure vanilla extract

4 oz cream cheese, at room temperature

¼ cup Strawberry Compote (page 152)

TASTEMAKER TIP:

To achieve perfectly round cookies—right after taking them out of the oven (before transferring to a cooling area), I gently swirl the ring of a mason jar (making sure it's bigger than the cookies) around each cookie 2–3 times.

A delicious variation of strawberry cheesecake. Cheesecake is one of my favorite sweets, and these cookies do not disappoint. Allow time for them to cool before enjoying. The puddles of cream cheese can easily burn the roof of your mouth if you're too eager—I'm speaking from experience.

Preheat the oven to 350°F (180°C).

In a medium bowl, whisk together the flour, 1 cup of graham cracker crumbs, and the baking soda. Set aside.

In a another medium bowl, using a handheld electric mixer, beat together the butter, granulated sugar, brown sugar, and salt on medium speed until well combined and fluffy, about 2 minutes.

Add the egg and vanilla and beat until well combined, about 30 seconds. With the mixer on low speed, slowly add the flour mixture. Using a rubber spatula, scrape down the sides of the bowl and fold all the ingredients together.

In a separate large bowl, combine the cream cheese and compote. Mash together with a fork until slightly swirled together. You do not want your mixture to be completely light pink in color.

Using a 1-ounce scoop (2 tablespoons), make the cookie dough balls and place them on the prepared baking sheets, spacing the dough balls evenly, about 2 inches apart. Press the cookie dough balls down slightly into thick disks, then use the back of a tablespoon to create an indentation in the center of each dough disk. Spoon about 2 heaping teaspoons of cream cheese filling into each indentation, dividing evenly between the cookies. Sprinkle with the remaining 1–2 tablespoons of graham cracker crumbs, if you like.

Bake the cookies, 1 sheet at a time, until golden brown, crispy on the outside and soft on the inside (I won't argue this), about 12 minutes. Transfer the baking sheet to a wire rack and let the cookies cool on the baking sheet for 3 minutes, then, using a metal spatula, carefully transfer the cookies from the baking sheet to the rack to cool completely.

S'MORES DIP

1 tablespoon unsalted butter

1 bag (12 oz) milk or semisweet chocolate chips

7 oz regular marshmallows (about 30 marshmallows)

Graham crackers for dipping

I'm always looking for something good and easy when it comes to desserts. Hand to God—I'm not the *best* baker, but I'm working on it. However, this S'mores Dip is an easy and delicious dessert for anyone to make. Minimal prep time, minimal ingredients, and maximum flavor.

Position a rack in the upper third of the oven and preheat it to 375°F (190°C). Place an 8-inch round cake pan in the oven to warm.

Remove the warm pan from the oven. Put the butter in the pan and swirl to coat the bottom. When the butter is melted, add the chocolate chips in an even layer. Top the chocolate chips with the marshmallows in an even layer.

Bake until the chocolate is melted and the marshmallows are lightly golden brown, about 12 minutes.

Serve right away with the graham crackers for dipping.

PEAR SPICE CAKE WITH BOURBON GLAZE

MAKES 6–8 SERVINGS

FOR THE CAKE

1 lb ripe Bartlett or Bosc pears, peeled, cored, and chopped

½ cup granulated sugar, divided

¼ cup water

1 tablespoon fresh lemon juice

Cooking spray

½ cup firmly packed light brown sugar

⅔ cup avocado oil

2 large eggs

1 teaspoon pure vanilla extract

1 cup all-purpose flour

1 teaspoon baking powder

½ teaspoon baking soda

1 teaspoon ground cinnamon

1 teaspoon ground ginger

½ teaspoon ground allspice

½ teaspoon ground nutmeg

½ teaspoon kosher salt

FOR THE GLAZE

2 oz bourbon

1 small cinnamon stick

1 cup confectioners' sugar

½ teaspoon pure vanilla extract

Pinch salt

This spice cake endured plenty of trial and error to reach its current state of success. It is sweet, moist, and simply delicious. The bourbon glaze is one of the details that makes this cake sing. I swoon over the richness of the bourbon, which is paired with the sweet-salty balance of salt, cinnamon, sugar, and vanilla.

To make the cake, in a medium saucepan over medium heat, combine the pears, ¼ cup granulated sugar, the water, and lemon juice. Cook, stirring occasionally, until the pear is softened, about 7 minutes. Transfer the mixture to a blender and process to a smooth puree. You should have 1½ cups of puree. Transfer the puree to a medium bowl and let cool for 10 minutes.

Preheat the oven to 350°F (180°C). Grease a 9 x 5-inch loaf pan lightly with cooking spray, then line it with parchment paper so that two edges come up and over the longer edges of the pan.

Add the remaining ¼ cup of granulated sugar, the brown sugar, avocado oil, eggs, and vanilla to the bowl of pear puree and whisk to combine.

In another medium bowl, whisk together the flour, baking powder, baking soda, cinnamon, ginger, allspice, nutmeg, and salt. Add the flour mixture to the pear mixture and stir to combine.

Pour the batter into the prepared loaf pan and smooth the top. Bake for 50–55 minutes, until golden brown and a toothpick inserted into the center of the cake comes out clean. Transfer to a wire rack and let cool in the pan for 10 minutes. Then, using the parchment as handles, remove the cake from the pan. Peel away the parchment and let the cake cool completely.

While the cake bakes, make the glaze. In a small saucepan over medium heat, combine the bourbon and cinnamon stick. Simmer, stirring occasionally, until the bourbon is reduced by half, about 3-4 minutes. Remove from the heat and let cool completely. Remove the cinnamon stick. Add the confectioners' sugar, vanilla, and salt and whisk until smooth.

When the cake is cooled, brush the glaze over the top and sides of the cake. Let stand until the glaze sets, about 30 minutes. Slice and serve.

CREAMY NO-BAKE CHEESECAKE BITES

MAKES 9–10 SERVINGS

1 package (7 oz) crisp butter cookies, such as Pepperidge Farm Chessmen Butter Cookies (about 24 cookies)

4 tablespoons unsalted butter or vanilla bean ghee, melted

1 tablespoon sugar

¼ teaspoon kosher salt

1 (16 oz) package cream cheese, at room temperature

1 can (14 oz) sweetened condensed milk

1 tablespoon fresh lemon juice

2 teaspoons pure vanilla extract

A no-bake dessert feels like a relief, an exhale, a reward if you will. Achieving these creamy and delicious bites without turning on an oven or stove brings me so much joy. If you are hosting, this is a great dessert to prepare and refrigerate while you finish getting ready for your guests.

Place the butter cookies in a food processor and process into fine crumbs. Transfer the cookie crumbs to a medium bowl and stir in the butter, sugar, and salt until the mixture looks like wet sand.

Line 16 cups of 2 (12-cup) cupcake pans with paper or foil liners. Add 1 packed heaping tablespoon of the cookie crumb mixture to each cup. Use a small glass to press the cookie crumbs into an even, solid layer.

Wipe out the bowl of the food processor and add the cream cheese, condensed milk, lemon juice, and vanilla. Process until smooth, then transfer the cream-cheese mixture into a piping bag fitted with a large plain tip or a zip-top plastic bag with the corner snipped off.

Pipe the cheesecake filling into the prepared cups, filling them about two-thirds full. Refrigerate until set, at least 4 hours, or up to 2 days in advance. Serve.

TASTEMAKER TIP: *To make these into blueberry cheesecake bites, prepare the blueberry compote on page 139 and let it cool completely. Add 1 heaping tablespoon of the compote to the top of each mini cheesecake. Refrigerate as directed. If you like, reserve about ¼ cup of the cookie crumb mixture and sprinkle it over the top of the cheesecakes just before serving.*

SALTED CARAMEL PRETZEL BLONDIES

MAKES 9 SERVINGS

FOR THE SALTED CARAMEL

1 cup granulated sugar

1 teaspoon light corn syrup

3 tablespoons water

6 tablespoons unsalted butter, cut into pieces

½ cup heavy cream

½ teaspoon kosher salt

¼ teaspoon pure vanilla extract

FOR THE BLONDIES

Cooking spray

½ cup unsalted butter, at room temperature

1 cup firmly packed dark brown sugar

⅛ teaspoon baking soda

½ teaspoon baking powder

1 large egg, at room temperature

1 teaspoon pure vanilla extract

¼ teaspoon kosher salt

1 cup all-purpose flour

½ cup coarsely crumbled mini pretzels

Vanilla ice cream for serving

We all know blondies are brownies' favorite cousin. These Salted Caramel Blondies can easily make you feel like you have this baking thing down pat. They are a dream of salty and sweet. The pretzel crumble adds a delightful crunch to the soft and chewy blondie.

To make the salted caramel, in a medium-size deep saucepan over medium heat, combine the granulated sugar, corn syrup, and water. Stir until the mixture is just evenly moistened. Use a pastry brush dipped in water to brush down the sides of the saucepan (this helps prevent sugar crystals from messing up the caramel). Bring the sugar to a boil, occasionally swirling the pan for even cooking, but do not stir. Cook until the sugar turns caramel brown, about 5 minutes, then remove the saucepan from the heat.

Carefully add the butter, stirring to combine; the butter will foam. Once the butter is completely stirred in, slowly add the heavy cream. Stir in the salt and vanilla. Set aside (still off the heat) while you make the blondie batter; if the caramel gets too thick, warm it gently over low heat. You'll have about 1⅓ cups of caramel.

To make the blondies, preheat the oven to 375°F (190°C). Lightly grease an 8-inch square baking dish with cooking spray, then line it with a piece of parchment paper so that 2 edges come up and over the sides. Lightly grease the parchment with cooking spray.

In a large bowl, combine the butter and brown sugar. Use a handheld electric mixer fitted with the beater attachments. Set it on medium-low speed and beat the butter and brown sugar together until light and fluffy, about 3 minutes. Scrape down the bowl with a rubber spatula. Add the baking soda, baking powder, egg, vanilla, and salt and beat on medium speed until well combined, about 1 minute. Scrape down the sides of the bowl. Stir in the flour until just combined. The batter will be thick.

Scrape the batter into the prepared baking dish and spread into an even layer. Drizzle about 2 tablespoons of the caramel over the top of the batter. Press the pretzels into the top of the batter so they are evenly spaced.

Bake until the blondies are golden brown and a toothpick inserted into the center comes out clean, about 25 minutes.

Transfer the dish to a wire rack and let cool completely in the dish. When the blondies are cool, remove them using the parchment paper. Transfer to a cutting board and cut into squares. Rewarm the remaining caramel sauce. Serve with vanilla ice cream drizzled with caramel sauce.

BLUEBERRY-COMPOTE BUTTER-CRUNCH CAKE

MAKES 4-6 SERVINGS

FOR THE
BLUEBERRY COMPOTE

1 lb fresh blueberries

¾ cup sugar

1 tablespoon cornstarch

1 tablespoon cold water

2 teaspoons fresh lemon juice

½ teaspoon finely grated
lemon zest

FOR THE CAKE

1 cup all-purpose flour

⅔ cup sugar

1½ teaspoons baking powder

¾ teaspoon kosher salt

¾ cup whole milk

1 teaspoon pure vanilla extract

Vanilla ice cream for serving

I love the sticky, crunchy bottom and sides of a cake. This Butter Crunch Cake gives you a bit of that sensation in each bite. I adore it with the Blueberry Compote, but it also goes well with Strawberry Compote (page 152), Honey Butter (page 41), or just plain. Any way you serve it, it's always delicious.

To make the blueberry compote, in a medium saucepan over medium heat, combine the blueberries and sugar. Cook, stirring occasionally, until the sugar melts and the blueberries break down, about 6 minutes.

In a small bowl, whisk together the cornstarch, water, lemon juice, and lemon zest. Add the mixture to the blueberries and cook, stirring, until thickened, about 3 minutes. Remove from the heat and set aside to cool while you make the cake. You'll have about 2 cups of compote.

To make the cake, preheat the oven to 375°F (190°C). Place the butter in a 9 x 5-inch loaf pan and put it in the oven on the center rack to melt, about 3–4 minutes, then remove the pan from the oven.

Meanwhile, in a large bowl, whisk together the flour, sugar, baking powder, and salt. Whisk in the milk and vanilla extract until smooth. The mixture should resemble pancake batter.

Slowly pour the batter over the butter in the loaf pan.

Dollop about ⅓ cup of blueberry compote over the batter.

Using a butter knife, swirl the blueberry compote into the butter. You should see streaks of butter and compote swirling through the batter.

Bake until the cake is golden and a toothpick inserted into the center comes out clean, 40–45 minutes.

Let cool on a wire rack for at least 10 minutes. Serve warm in scoops or directly from the loaf pan with ice cream and additional blueberry compote.

CRISPY CORNFLAKE SQUARES

**MAKES 9–12 SERVINGS;
9 LARGE SQUARES
OR 12 BARS**

Cooking spray

4 tablespoons unsalted butter

1 bag (10 oz) mini
marshmallows

¼ teaspoon kosher salt

7 heaping cups cornflakes
(about 9½ oz)

Imagine if you combined a Rice Krispy Treat and a marshmallow dream bar from Starbucks—these Crispy Cornflake Squares would be the result. If you *really* have a sweet tooth, you can change the 7 cups of regular cornflakes to 6 cups of frosted cornflakes to add a little extra sweetness.

Line a 9-inch-square baking dish with parchment paper, ensuring that the parchment hangs over the edge on all sides, and lightly grease with cooking spray.

In a large saucepan over medium-low heat, melt the butter. Add the marshmallows and salt. Using a silicone spatula, stir the mixture until the marshmallows melt and the mixture is well combined. Quickly stir in the cornflakes, stirring well to combine.

Scrape the mixture into the prepared baking dish. Grease the bottom of a flat glass with cooking spray and use it to press the mixture firmly into a dense, even layer. Let cool completely, about 30 minutes.

Remove the treats from the pan using the edges of the parchment. Transfer to a cutting board, peel away and discard the parchment, and cut into 9 squares or 12 bars.

BISCUIT DOUGHNUTS WITH LEMON GLAZE

MAKES 8 SERVINGS

Vegetable oil for frying

1 package (16 oz) large refrigerator biscuits (there should be 8 biscuits)

1 cup confectioners' sugar

1 teaspoon finely grated lemon zest

5 teaspoons fresh-squeezed lemon juice, or as needed

These Biscuit Doughnuts are very beginner-friendly—I came up with them before I even owned a stand mixer. The Lemon Glaze for your finished doughnuts is simple, smooth, and zesty. It lifts these sweet treats to the next level and wraps them in a delicate glaze. They are best the day they are made.

Fill a large, deep frying pan with 2 inches of vegetable oil (the pan should not be more than half full). Over medium-high heat, warm the oil until a deep-frying thermometer registers 365–370°F (185–188°C). Place a wire rack lined with paper towels next to the stovetop.

While the oil heats, using a ¾–1 inch round cutter, cut out the center of each biscuit. You can fry these as doughnut holes or discard them.

In a medium bowl, combine the confectioners' sugar, lemon zest, and lemon juice. Whisk to combine; the glaze should be just thick enough to run off the spoon easily.

When the oil is hot, working in batches, fry 2–3 doughnuts in the oil, turning once or twice with tongs, until deep golden brown and cooked through, about 3 minutes total. Transfer them to the prepared rack to drain. While you are frying, keep a close eye on the temperature and adjust the heat up or down as needed to keep the temperature of the oil as consistent as possible. Repeat to fry all the doughnuts. If frying the holes, watch them carefully, as they only take about 1 minute.

When the doughnuts are cooled but still slightly warm, dip 1 side into the glaze, letting any excess drip off. Place the doughnuts back on the rack, glazed-side up, and let cool completely so the glaze sets.

Sauces, Dressings & Garnishes

GINGER SIMPLE SYRUP 143

CREAMY JERK SAUCE 145

GARLIC BUTTER SAUCE 146

ROASTED GARLIC CAESAR DRESSING 147

SUN-DRIED TOMATO AIOLI 149

PERFECT ROASTED GARLIC 150

SCOTCH BONNET AIOLI 151

STRAWBERRY COMPOTE 152

CHIPOLTE SAUCE 155

JAMAICAN GREEN SEASONING 156

SEAFOOD STOCK 158

CHICKEN STOCK 159

GINGER SIMPLE SYRUP

MAKES 1 CUP

¾ cup granulated sugar

½ cup firmly packed dark brown sugar

1¼ cup distilled water

4–5 whole allspice berries

2½–inch piece fresh ginger, peeled

This Ginger Simple Syrup tastes fresh and is not too thick, as some store-bought syrups can be. It is a great boost for your cocktails or mocktails. Try it with the Island Ting (page 28). You can also make a fresh homemade ginger ale by adding this syrup to a glass of regular club soda.

In a medium saucepan over medium-high heat, completely dissolve the granulated sugar and brown sugar in the water, stirring constantly.

Add the allspice and ginger and bring to a gentle boil, stirring occasionally. Cook and stir for 2 minutes, then reduce the heat to low to maintain a low simmer, cover, and cook for 15 minutes longer, until syrup-like consistency is formed.

Remove the pan from the heat for at least 1 hour.

Once cooled, pour the syrup into an airtight mason jar or glass bottle.

Store in the refrigerator for up to 14 days.

CREAMY JERK SAUCE

MAKES ½ CUP

2 teaspoons butter

1 cup half-and-half

1 tablespoon jerk seasoning,
such as Walkerswood

1 teaspoon YardSpice
(substitution, page 13)

1 teaspoon WhiteSpice
(substitution, page 13)

1 teaspoon CajunSpice
(substitution, page 13)

This creamy sauce offers the delicious flavors of jerk seasoning, while taming some of its fiery kick. The possibilities for this sauce are endless. Try it with the Jerk Chicken Burrito (page 52), on your favorite salad, or drizzled over an assortment of cooked vegetables.

Place the butter in a medium saucepan over medium heat and melt it. Add the half-and-half, jerk seasoning, YardSpice, WhiteSpice, and CajunSpice.

Mix well and cook until the sauce has a thick and creamy consistency, about 3–4 minutes.

Serve immediately.

GARLIC BUTTER SAUCE

MAKES 1 CUP

¾ cup butter

2 heads Perfect Roasted Garlic with cooking oil (page 150)

½ cup chopped fresh flat-leaf parsley

1 cup Chicken Stock (page 159) or white wine

1 tablespoon WhiteSpice (substitution, page 13)

1 teaspoon salt

This garlic butter sauce is perfect on Chicken Meatballs (page 84), pan-seared salmon, steaks, and most poultry dishes. One of my favorite uses for this sauce is to pour it over fresh pasta and add a bit of salt and black pepper. You have a delicious pasta meal in minutes.

In a large skillet over medium-low heat, melt the butter. Squeeze in the roasted garlic along with the residual oil (about 2 tablespoons) and mix well while trying to smooth out the garlic chunks.

Once the garlic is as smooth as you can get it, add the parsley and stock. Raise the heat to medium-high.

Season with WhiteSpice and salt, and cook for about 3 minutes, allowing the ingredients to combine.

Store in an airtight container in the refrigerator for 2–3 days.

ROASTED GARLIC CAESAR DRESSING

MAKES 1 CUP

3 anchovy fillets in oil

2 heads Perfect Roasted Garlic (page 150)

2 eggs yolks, at room temperature

1 tablespoon Dijon mustard

Juice of 1 small lemon

1 tablespoon finely grated lemon zest

¼ cup grated Parmesan cheese

¼ cup grated Asiago cheese

2 teaspoons WhiteSpice (substitution, page 13)

1 tablespoon freshly ground black pepper

½ tablespoon Maldon sea salt

¼ cup olive oil

¼ cup avocado oil

In my eyes, Caesar dressing is already the elite dressing. The roasted garlic and seasonings in this recipe enhance the dressing even more. It is creamy and simple. Toss with your favorite greens and enjoy, or be like me, and eat it with your pizza crust!

In a large bowl—ideally your serving bowl—mash together the anchovy fillets and garlic. Add the egg yolks, mustard, and lemon juice and zest, and whisk to combine. Add the Parmesan, Asiago, WhiteSpice, pepper, and salt. Pour in the olive oil in a steady stream, slowly whisking as you go. Do the same with the avocado oil.

Serve immediately, or store in an airtight container in the refrigerator for up to 7 days.

SUN-DRIED TOMATO AIOLI

MAKES ½ CUP

¼ cup sun-dried tomatoes in olive oil

1 clove Perfect Roasted Garlic (page 150)

4 fresh basil leaves, chopped

1 tablespoon fresh-squeezed lemon juice

1 tablespoon water

½ cup mayonnaise

1½ teaspoons sugar

I put this sh*t on *everything*! I'm aware that I may have a special obsession with sun-dried tomatoes, but this aioli is truly delicious. Sun-dried tomatoes have a naturally unique flavor that balances both tart and sweet. Try this aioli as a dip with fresh vegetables or crispy French fries.

In a blender, combine the sun-dried tomatoes, garlic, basil, lemon juice, and water and blend until smooth.

Add the mayonnaise to a medium bowl and pour in the sun-dried tomato mixture. Top with the sugar (this balances the acidity) and mix well until the sugar is dissolved and all ingredients are smoothly combined.

Store in an airtight container in the refrigerator for 2–3 days.

PERFECT ROASTED GARLIC

**MAKES 1 BULB OF
ROASTED GARLIC**

1 head garlic

1 teaspoon butter

2–3 tablespoons olive oil

When I first started cooking, adding roasted garlic to everything was a trick I used to seem savvy in the kitchen. While my skills have grown and expanded quite a bit since then, I still believe a good bulb of roasted garlic adds depth to a multitude of dishes, sauces, and dressings.

Preheat the oven to 400°F (200°C).

Trim off the top of the head of garlic to expose the cloves and place it on a sheet of aluminum foil. Add the butter and drizzle with the olive oil, evenly coating the garlic. Close the foil tightly and place on a rimmed baking sheet.

Bake for 50–60 minutes, until fragrant and softened. For more caramelized garlic, reduce the heat to 325°F (170°C) and bake for an additional 15–20 minutes. Use right away.

TASTEMAKER TIP: *Adding a fresh thyme sprig takes the garlic to another level and is great for presentation.*

SCOTCH BONNET AIOLI

MAKES 1 CUP

1 Scotch bonnet pepper, seeded and chopped

2 cloves garlic

1 tablespoon water

2 teaspoons honey

1 teaspoon Dijon mustard

¼ cup mayonnaise

2 tablespoons ketchup

¼ teaspoon salt

This aioli packs a serious heat punch to your taste buds. The scotch bonnet pepper is similar to the habanero pepper in taste. It has lots of heat and a subtle sweetness and is commonly used in Jamaican cuisine. The heat of this creamy condiment is real, but so is the explosive flavor.

In a food processor or blender, combine the Scotch bonnet, garlic, water, honey and mustard and process until smooth.

In a small bowl, combine the mayonnaise, ketchup, and blended mixture. Add the salt and whisk together until smooth and evenly combined.

Store in an airtight container in the refrigerator for up to 7 days.

STRAWBERRY COMPOTE

MAKES 2 CUPS

Juice and finely grated zest of
1 large orange

Juice and finely grated zest of
1 small lemon

1 teaspoon cornstarch

2 cups diced strawberries

½ cup sugar

1 tablespoon water (optional)

Making your own compote is an important and useful skill to have in the kitchen. Cutting the strawberries neat and petite for this recipe will make it more appealing to the eye. Also, adding orange zest deepens the flavor profile and gives it that little something extra. Try this on breakfast biscuits, in cake mixes, or on toast.

In a medium bowl, combine the orange juice, lemon juice, and cornstarch to create a slurry. Set aside.

Place the strawberries and sugar in a medium saucepan over medium heat. Cook and stir gently for 2 minutes. You'll see a lot of liquid pooling and the strawberries starting to break down.

Add the slurry mixture, along with the orange and lemon zest. Mix well.

If the strawberries aren't juicy enough, add the water.

Continue cooking and stirring until you get a thick jam-like consistency, about 10–15 minutes. Remove from the heat and transfer the compote to a heat-safe bowl. Allow the compote to cool completely.

Store in an airtight container in the refrigerator for up to 7 days.

CHIPOTLE SAUCE

MAKES 1 CUP

6 chipotle chiles in adobo

Juice and finely grated zest of
1 small lime

3 tablespoons honey

1 tablespoon water

1 tablespoon white vinegar

⅓ cup mayonnaise

This isn't your average chipotle mayo, let's get that clear. The taste is more satisfying than any store-bought alternative. She's sweet, creamy, spicy, and smooth all at the same time. She's layered and very easy to make. Drizzle over your favorite burger or salad.

In a blender, combine the chipotles, lime juice and zest, honey, water, vinegar, and mayonnaise and blend until smooth and evenly combined. Store in an airtight container in the refrigerator for 2–3 days.

TASTEMAKER TIP: *For more of a Southwest-style sauce, add ⅓ cup ranch dressing.*

JAMAICAN GREEN SEASONING

MAKES 2 CUPS

1 Scotch bonnet chile

8 cloves garlic, peeled

6 large fresh basil leaves

15–20 fresh thyme sprigs

4–5 green onions, ends trimmed, cut in half

1 cup lightly packed fresh chives

1 cup lightly packed chopped fresh flat-leaf parsley

½ cup lightly packed fresh dill

¼ cup firmly packed brown sugar

1-inch piece fresh ginger, peeled and sliced

1 small shallot, cubed

1 large red bell pepper, cubed

1 large green bell pepper, cubed

2 tablespoons whole peppercorn

2 tablespoons whole allspice

2 tablespoons salt

Green seasoning is a kitchen staple for many cooks in the Caribbean islands. I use green seasoning in everything—oxtail, curry, soup, and stew. Make sure to wash all the herbs and vegetables thoroughly. Forgetting to do so could result in a gritty sauce, and no one wants that.

Place all the ingredients in a food processor. Process on high speed until smooth and evenly combined.

Store in an airtight container in the refrigerator for up to 14 days.

SEAFOOD STOCK

MAKES 1 QUART

3 tablespoons olive oil

4 lobster shells

Shells from 1 lb shrimp

6 ribs celery, halved with the leaves

2 large carrots, quartered and unpeeled

1 large yellow onion, diced

1 head garlic, halved crosswise

½ cup dry white wine

10 fresh thyme sprigs

6 whole allspice berries

3 bay leaves

2 tablespoons whole peppercorn

8 cups water

2 tablespoons salt

Making your own stock is an absolute game changer. It can save you money and it's also a great way to incorporate sustainability practices into your cooking—especially if you use leftover scraps, such as carrot peel, celery leaves, seafood shells, and garlic and onion skins.

In a large stockpot, or the biggest pot you have, over medium-high heat, warm the olive oil. Add the lobster and shrimp shells and cook for 2–3 minutes, until they become pink in color and very fragrant. Add the celery, carrots, onion, and garlic. Cook for 5–6 minutes longer, until softened.

Add the wine and deglaze the pan, scraping up any bits on the bottom. Cook for 3–4 minutes to reduce the wine a bit, then add the thyme, allspice, bay leaves, and peppercorns. Mix, then add the water. Reduce the heat to low and simmer for 45–60 minutes, until reduced and fragrant.

Remove from the heat and allow the stock to cool fully. Add the salt and strain the stock through a fine-mesh strainer lined with cheesecloth. Be sure to press out all the liquid using the back of a spoon or a spatula.

Divide into deli containers and refrigerate for up to 7 days or freeze for up to 6 months.

CHICKEN STOCK

MAKES 3–4 QUARTS

1 roasted chicken carcass

4–6 ribs celery, halved with the leaves

2 large carrots, halved and unpeeled

1 large yellow onion, halved with the skin on

1 head garlic, halved with the skin on

1 cup DinnerPlus Brining Blend (substitution, page 13)

10 fresh thyme sprigs

4 fresh rosemary sprigs

2 bay leaves

5 quarts water

I'm hoping you've landed here because you made the Jump-Start Chicken (page 87) and wanted to put that carcass to good use! The beauty of chicken stock is that it is much more versatile than a seafood or beef stock because the chicken flavor doesn't overpower a dish in anyway.

In a large stockpot over medium-high heat, combine the carcass, celery, carrots, onion, garlic, Brining Blend, thyme, rosemary, and bay leaves. Cover with the water and bring to a boil. Reduce the heat to low to maintain a simmer and cook, uncovered, for 2–3 hours, skimming any foamy impurities as they come up, until you are left with a translucent broth.

Remove from the heat and let the stock cool fully. Strain the stock through a colander and then again through a fine-mesh strainer lined with cheesecloth. Be sure to press out all the liquid using the back of a spoon or a spatula.

Divide into deli containers and refrigerate for up to 7 days or freeze for up to 6 months.

INDEX

A

Aioli
Scotch Bonnet Aioli, 151
Sun-Dried Tomato Aioli, 149

Allspice
Ginger Simple Syrup, 143
Jamaican Rum Punch, 25
Sorrel Margarita, 21
Yard Toddy, 29

Appetizers & all-day meals
Bougie Chopped Cheese
Sliders, 55
Caesar Toast, 57
Caramelized Shallot & Roasted
Garlic Lobster Bisque, 59
Chorizo Taco Cups, 49
Crab Rangoon Dip, 65
Elevated Snack Wraps, 62
Garlic Lemon Pepper Wings, 50
Hot Honey Crispy Shrimp, 60
Jerk Chicken Burrito, 52
Mason Jar Noodle Soup, 53
Mustard Chicken Bites, 63
Sticky Fried Short Ribs, 56

Artichoke & Spinach Zucchini
Boats, 118

Asparagus
Orzo Salad, 116
Steak-Wrapped Asparagus, 121

B

Bacon
BBL Fried Cabbage, 93
Boosted Breakfast Bowl, 111
Breakfast Casserole, 44
Jump-Start Chicken, 87

Basil Spritz, 23

BBL Fried Cabbage, 93

Beans
Boosted Breakfast Bowl, 111

Cauliflower Southwest Skillet
with Chipotle Sauce, 112
Chickpea Cook Up, 38
Jamaican Oxtail, 81–82
Jamaican Rice & "Peas" (From a
Can), 77
Lemongrass Ground Turkey, 117

Beef
Bougie Chopped Cheese
Sliders, 55
Jamaican Oxtail, 81–82
Steak-Wrapped Asparagus, 121
Sticky Fried Short Ribs, 56

Biscuit Doughnuts with Lemon
Glaze, 141

Black-Eyed Peas, 105

Blondies, Salted Caramel Pretzel,
136

Blueberry Compote Butter Crunch
Cake, 139

Bok Choy, Garlic-Ginger, 127

Bourbon Glaze, Pear Spice Cake
with, 134

Branzino, Turmeric-Ginger, 96

Breads
Baked Egg Bread Bowl, 36
Caesar Toast, 57
Jammy Eggs & Honey Butter
Toast, 45
Toasted Brioche with Cream
Cheese & Strawberry
Compote, 35

Breakfast & brunch
Baked Egg Bread Bowl, 36
Boosted Breakfast Bowl, 111
Breakfast Casserole, 44
Breakfast Pockets, 39
Callaloo & Saltfish Fritters, 42
Chickpea Cook Up, 38
Honey Butter Cornbread

Waffle, 41
Jammy Eggs & Honey Butter
Toast, 45
Toasted Brioche with Cream
Cheese & Strawberry
Compote, 35

Brining Blend substitute, 13

Broccoli
Callaloo Stew, 115

Burger, Sweet Sausage Smash, 78

Burrito, Jerk Chicken, 52

Butter
Brown Butter Tortellini, 89
Garlic Butter Sauce, 146
Honey Butter Cornbread
Waffle, 41
Jammy Eggs & Honey Butter
Toast, 45

C

Cabbage
BBL Fried Cabbage, 93
Jamaican Steamed Cabbage,
126

Caesar Dressing, Roasted Garlic,
147

Caesar Toast, 57

CajunSpice substitute, 13

Cakes
Blueberry Compote Butter
Crunch Cake, 139
Pear Spice Cake with Bourbon
Glaze, 134

Callaloo
Callaloo & Saltfish Fritters, 42
Callaloo Stew, 115

Caramel, Salted, Pretzel Blondies,
136

Cauliflower Southwest Skillet with
Chipotle Sauce, 112

Cheese. See also Cream cheese
    Bougie Chopped Cheese
        Sliders, 55
    Breakfast Casserole, 44
    Breakfast Pockets, 39
    Caesar Toast, 57
    Cauliflower Southwest Skillet
        with Chipotle Sauce, 112
    Chorizo Taco Cups, 49
    Crab Rangoon Dip, 65
    Elevated Snack Wraps, 62
    Grilled Halloumi Salad with
        Tahini Dressing, 123
    Jerk Chicken Burrito, 52
    Jerk Mac & Cheese with
        Creamy Jerk Sauce, 75–76
    Roasted Garlic Caesar
        Dressing, 147
    Sausage & Sun-Dried Tomato
        Stuffed Shells, 71–72
    Spinach & Artichoke Zucchini
        Boats, 118
    Sweet Sausage Smash Burger,
        78
    Three Sauce Naan Pizza with
        Crispy Prosciutto, 95
Cheesecake Bites, Creamy No-
    Bake, 135
Chicken
    Brown Stew Chicken, 83
    Chicken Meatballs with Garlic
        Butter Sauce & Orzo Salad,
        84
    Chicken Stock, 159
Chickpeas
    Chickpea Cook Up, 38
    Lemongrass Ground Turkey, 117
Chiles
    Chipotle Sauce, 155
    Jamaican Green Seasoning, 156

Chipotle Sauce, 155
Chocolate
    S'mores Dip, 132
Cocktails
    Basil Spritz, 23
    Brunch Punch, 17
    Island Ting, 28
    Jamaican Rum Punch, 25
    Paloma-Ann, 22
    Smoke & Berry, 18
    Sorrel Margarita, 21
    Tamarind Margarita, 26
    Tea-Tini, 30
    Yard Toddy, 29
Cookies, Strawberry Cheesecake,
    131
Corn
    Cauliflower Southwest Skillet
        with Chipotle Sauce, 112
    Jerk Chicken Burrito, 52
Cornbread Waffle, Honey Butter,
    41
Cornflake Squares, Crispy, 140
Cornmeal. See Cornbread Waffle
Crab
    Crab Rangoon Dip, 65
    Cucumber Crab Rounds, 122
    Gochujang Crab Noodles, 90
Cranberries
    Smoke & Berry, 18
Cream cheese
    Crab Rangoon Dip, 65
    Creamy No-Bake Cheesecake
        Bites, 135
    Strawberry Cheesecake
        Cookies, 131
    Toasted Brioche with Cream
        Cheese & Strawberry
        Compote, 35
Cucumbers

Cucumber Crab Rounds, 122
Grilled Halloumi Salad with
    Tahini Dressing, 123

D
Desserts
    Biscuit Doughnuts with Lemon
        Glaze, 141
    Blueberry Compote Butter
        Crunch Cake, 139
    Creamy No-Bake Cheesecake
        Bites, 135
    Crispy Cornflake Squares, 140
    Pear Spice Cake with Bourbon
        Glaze, 134
    Salted Caramel Pretzel
        Blondies, 136
    S'mores Dip, 132
    Strawberry Cheesecake
        Cookies, 131
Dinner Plus spices, 13
Dips
    Crab Rangoon Dip, 65
    Scotch Bonnet Aioli, 151
    S'mores Dip, 132
    Sun-Dried Tomato Aioli, 149
Doughnuts, Biscuit, with Lemon
    Glaze, 141
Dressing, Roasted Garlic Caesar,
    147

E
Eggs
    Baked Egg Bread Bowl, 36
    Boosted Breakfast Bowl, 111
    Breakfast Casserole, 44
    Breakfast Pockets, 39
    Jammy Eggs & Honey Butter
        Toast, 45

F
Fish
    Callaloo & Saltfish Fritters, 42
    Crab Rangoon Dip, 65
    Turmeric-Ginger Branzino, 96
Fritters
    Callaloo & Saltfish Fritters, 42
    Zucchini & Green Onion
        Fritters, 125

G
Garlic
    Caramelized Shallot & Roasted
        Garlic Lobster Bisque, 59
    Chicken Meatballs with Garlic
        Butter Sauce & Orzo Salad,
        84
    Garlic Butter Sauce, 146
    Garlic-Ginger Bok Choy, 127
    Garlicky Lemon Pepper Lamb
        Chops with Honey Glaze, 99
    Perfect Roasted Garlic, 150
    Roasted Garlic Caesar
        Dressing, 147
    Scotch Bonnet Aioli, 151
    Sun-Dried Tomato Aioli, 149
Ginger
    Basil Spritz, 23
    Garlic-Ginger Bok Choy, 127
    Ginger Simple Syrup, 143
    Island Ting, 28
    Jamaican Rum Punch, 25
    Sorrel Margarita, 21
    Tamarind Margarita, 26
    Turmeric-Ginger Branzino, 96
Gochujang Crab Noodles, 90
Graham crackers
    S'mores Dip, 132
Grapefruit
    Paloma-Ann, 22
Green Onion & Zucchini Fritters,
    125

H
Herbs
    Basil Spritz, 23
    Jamaican Green Seasoning, 156
Hibiscus flower
    Sorrel Margarita, 21
Honey
    Garlicky Lemon Pepper Lamb
        Chops with Honey Glaze, 99
    Honey Butter Cornbread
        Waffle, 41
    Hot Honey Crispy Shrimp, 60
    Jammy Eggs & Honey Butter
        Toast, 45
    Tea-Tini, 30
    Yard Toddy, 29

I
Ingredients, pantry and kitchen, 11
Island Ting, 28

J
Jamaican Green Seasoning, 156
Jamaican Oxtail, 81–82
Jamaican Rice & "Peas", 77
Jamaican Rum Punch, 25
Jamaican Steamed Cabbage, 126
Jerk Chicken, Oven, 68
Jerk Chicken Burrito, 52
Jerk Mac & Cheese with Creamy
    Jerk Sauce, 75–76
Jerk Sauce, Creamy, 145

K
Kale
    Boosted Breakfast Bowl, 111
    Collard Kale with Smoked
        Turkey Neck Broth, 102
Kombucha
    Brunch Punch, 17

L
Lamb Chops, Garlicky Lemon
    Pepper, with Honey Glaze, 99
Lemon
    Biscuit Doughnuts with Lemon
        Glaze, 141
    Tea-Tini, 30
Lemongrass Ground Turkey, 117
Lettuce
    Caesar Toast, 57
Lime
    Paloma-Ann, 22
    Yard Toddy, 29
Lobster Bisque, Caramelized
    Shallot & Roasted Garlic, 59

M
Mango nectar
    Jamaican Rum Punch, 25
Maple Chicken & Rice, One-Pan,
    85
Margaritas
    Sorrel Margarita, 21
    Tamarind Margarita, 26
Marshmallows
    Crispy Cornflake Squares, 140
    S'mores Dip, 132
Meatballs, Chicken, with Garlic
    Butter Sauce & Orzo Salad, 84
Mezcal
    Smoke & Berry, 18
Mustard Chicken Bites, 63

O
Oh Wow spice substitutions, 13
Orange juice
    Brunch Punch, 17
    Jamaican Rum Punch, 25
Orzo Salad, 116
Oxtail, Jamaican, 81–82

P
Paloma-Ann, 22
Pantry ingredients, 11
Pasta and noodles
    Brown Butter Tortellini, 89
    Creamy Scallop Pappardelle, 73
    Gochujang Crab Noodles, 90
    Jerk Mac & Cheese with
        Creamy Jerk Sauce, 75–76
    Mason Jar Noodle Soup, 53
    Orzo Salad, 116
    Rasta Risotto, 88
    Sausage & Sun-Dried Tomato
        Stuffed Shells, 71–72
Pear Spice Cake with Bourbon
    Glaze, 134
Peas, Black-Eyed, 105
Peppers
    BBL Fried Cabbage, 93
    Callaloo & Saltfish Fritters, 42
    Callaloo Stew, 115
    Cauliflower Southwest Skillet
        with Chipotle Sauce, 112
    Chickpea Cook Up, 38
    Chipotle Sauce, 155
    Jamaican Green Seasoning, 156
    Jamaican Oxtail, 81–82
    Lemongrass Ground Turkey, 117
    One-Pan Maple Chicken &
        Rice, 85
    Rasta Risotto, 88
    Scotch Bonnet Aioli, 151
Pineapple juice
    Brunch Punch, 17
    Jamaican Rum Punch, 25
Pizza, Three Sauce Naan, with
    Crispy Prosciutto, 95
Pork. See Bacon; Prosciutto;
    Sausages
Potato hash browns
    Breakfast Casserole, 44
Pretzel Blondies, Salted Caramel,
    136
Prosciutto, Crispy, Three Sauce
    Naan Pizza with, 95

Prosecco
    Basil Spritz, 23
    Paloma-Ann, 22
Punch
    Brunch Punch, 17
    Jamaican Rum Punch, 25

R
Rasta Risotto, 88
Rice
    Holy Trinity Rice, 103
    Jamaican Rice & "Peas", 77
    One-Pan Maple Chicken &
        Rice, 85
Risotto, Rasta, 88
Rum
    Island Ting, 28
    Jamaican Rum Punch, 25
    Yard Toddy, 29

S
Salads
    Grilled Halloumi Salad with
        Tahini Dressing, 123
    Orzo Salad, 116
Saltfish & Callaloo Fritters, 42
Sauces
    Chipotle Sauce, 155
    Creamy Jerk Sauce, 145
    Garlic Butter Sauce, 146
    Scotch Bonnet Aioli, 151
    Sun-Dried Tomato Aioli, 149
Sausages
    Baked Egg Bread Bowl, 36
    BBL Fried Cabbage, 93
    Breakfast Casserole, 44
    Breakfast Pockets, 39
    Chorizo Taco Cups, 49
    Sausage & Sun-Dried Tomato
        Stuffed Shells, 71–72
    Sweet Sausage Smash Burger,
        78
Scallop Pappardelle, Creamy, 73
Scotch Bonnet Aioli, 151
Seafood. See also Fish; Shellfish

Seafood Stock, 158
Seasoning, Jamaican Green, 156
Shallot, Caramelized, & Roasted
    Garlic Lobster Bisque, 59
Shellfish
    Caramelized Shallot & Roasted
        Garlic Lobster Bisque, 59
    Creamy Scallop Pappardelle, 73
    Cucumber Crab Rounds, 122
    Gochujang Crab Noodles, 90
    Hot Honey Crispy Shrimp, 60
    Rasta Risotto, 88
Shrimp
    Hot Honey Crispy Shrimp, 60
    Rasta Risotto, 88
Simple Syrup, Ginger, 143
Sliders, Bougie Chopped Cheese,
    55
Smoke & Berry, 18
S'mores Dip, 132
Sorrel Margarita, 21
Soul Bowl Series, 100–106
Soups
    Caramelized Shallot & Roasted
        Garlic Lobster Bisque, 59
    Mason Jar Noodle Soup, 53
Spinach
    Baked Egg Bread Bowl, 36
    Breakfast Casserole, 44
    Chickpea Cook Up, 38
    Creamy Scallop Pappardelle, 73
    Gochujang Crab Noodles, 90
    Mason Jar Noodle Soup, 53
    Spinach & Artichoke Zucchini
        Boats, 118
Stew, Callaloo, 115
Stocks
    Chicken Stock, 159
    Seafood Stock, 158
Strawberries
    Strawberry Cheesecake
        Cookies, 131
    Strawberry Compote, 152
    Toasted Brioche with Cream
        Cheese & Strawberry

Compote, 35
Sweet Potatoes, Roasted, 104
Syrup, Ginger Simple, 143

T
Taco Cups, Chorizo, 49
Tahini Dressing, Grilled Halloumi
    Salad with, 123
Tamarind Margarita, 26
Tea-Tini, 30
Tequila
    Brunch Punch, 17
    Sorrel Margarita, 21
    Tamarind Margarita, 26
Ting
    Island Ting, 28
    Paloma-Ann, 22
Toast
    Caesar Toast, 57
    Jammy Eggs & Honey Butter
        Toast, 45
Tofu
    Mason Jar Noodle Soup, 53
Tomatoes
    Chickpea Cook Up, 38
    Grilled Halloumi Salad with
        Tahini Dressing, 123
    Jerk Chicken Burrito, 52
    Sausage & Sun-Dried Tomato
        Stuffed Shells, 71–72
    Sun-Dried Tomato Aioli, 149
Tortellini, Brown Butter, 89
Tortillas
    Chorizo Taco Cups, 49
    Elevated Snack Wraps, 62
    Jerk Chicken Burrito, 52
Turkey
    Black-Eyed Peas, 105
    Collard Kale with Smoked
        Turkey Neck Broth, 102
    Lemongrass Ground Turkey, 117
Turmeric-Ginger Branzino, 96

V
Vodka

Basil Spritz, 23
Paloma-Ann, 22
Tea-Tini, 30

W
Waffle, Honey Butter Cornbread,
    41
WhiteSpice substitute, 13
Wine. See Prosecco
Wraps, Elevated Snack, 62

Y
YardSpice substitute, 13
Yard Toddy, 29
Yuzu liqueur
    Basil Spritz, 23

Z
ZestySpice substitute, 13
Zucchini
    Spinach & Artichoke Zucchini
        Boats, 118
    Zucchini & Green Onion
        Fritters, 125

Acknowledgments

To my mother, Patricia, my first best friend, my support system, and my reason for everything I do, thank you for pushing me and being my first example of hard work and style.

To my sister Cayla, the pickiest eater I know. You've made it a challenge to feed you, but it helped hone my skills.

To my best friends Colin, Vandy, Dione, Toya, and Sean, who support me, critique me lovingly, and lift me up.

To my aunts, who are my true examples of cooking. My Aunty Sharon, who makes everything perfectly and has always been my example of trying new things in the kitchen. My Aunty Dawn, who makes the best soup, every Saturday, and has been my example of hard work and my first example of marriage and keeping a household. My Aunty Maureen, who makes the best barbecue pork and cabbage salad, my funniest aunty. My Aunty Hope, who doesn't eat pork but makes the best jerk pork on earth, a family party must-have.

To my clients past and present, thank you for the learning experiences, travels, and paychecks (lol).

To myself, for betting on you. For believing in you. For being your own shoulder to cry on. Sit with these moments and be present in them. You're doing great.

To my late Grandmother Zelda Graham. I signed this book deal a week following your passing. I couldn't wait to share the news with you, but I was just too late. Thank you for your guardianship, wisdom, and unconditional love. Thank you for championing me in the kitchen and being one of my first examples of the joy food brings.

weldon**owen**

an imprint of Insight Editions
P.O. Box 3088 San Rafael, CA 94912
www.weldonowen.com

CEO Raoul Goff
Publisher Roger Shaw
Publishing Director Katie Killebrew
Editor Kayla Belser
VP Creative Chrissy Kwasnik
VP Manufacturing Alix Nicholaeff
Sr Production Manager Joshua Smith
*Sr Production Manager, Subsidiary Right*s Lina s Palma-Temena

Photographer Biz Jones
Photography Assistant Samuel Orrego
Food Stylist Mira Evnine
Food Stylist Assistants Megan Litt & Anna Painter
Prop Stylist Elvis Maynard
Prop Stylist Assistant Todd Henry

Photographer for page 12: Shane Richards

Weldon Owen would also like to thank the following people for their work and support in producing this book:
Kim Laidlaw, Jessica Easto, Sean Garette, Blake Newby, Colin Welch, Margaret Parrish, and Elizabeth Parson.

Text © 2024 Scot Louie
Photography © Weldon Owen

ISBN: 979-8-88674-146-9

Manufactured in China by Insight Editions
10 9 8 7 6 5 4 3 2 1

Insight Editions, in association with Roots of Peace, will plant two trees for each tree used in the manufacturing of this
book. Roots of Peace is an internationally renowned humanitarian organization dedicated to eradicating land mines
worldwide and converting war-torn lands into productive farms and wildlife habitats. Roots of Peace will plant two million
fruit and nut trees in Afghanistan and provide farmers there with the skills and support necessary for sustainable land use.